Shivaji Park

Shivaji Park

Dadar 28: History, Places, People

SHANTA GOKHALE

SPEAKING
TIGER

SPEAKING TIGER BOOKS LLP
4381/4, Ansari Road, Daryaganj
New Delhi 110002

Published by Speaking Tiger Books in hardback 2020

ISBN: 978-81-944729-0-2
eISBN: 978-81-944729-1-9

10 9 8 7 6 5 4 3 2

Typeset in Cardo by SÜRYA, New Delhi
Printed at Chaman Enterprises, New Delhi

Contents

A commemorative pillar located on the kerb behind the Udyan Ganesh temple

Preface

I have lived in Shivaji Park for the greater part of eighty years. Writing a book about it should have been a three-month job. It has taken me a year. A place is like a person. The more you discover, the more there is to discover. I have made discoveries through books, novels, plays, conversations, interviews and, of course, by looking consciously at what had always been there to see. If I appear occasionally in this story it is as a resident, to contribute my memories and observations about the place.

This story of Shivaji Park begins with *Mahikavatichi Bakhar* (The Chronicle of Mahikavati), a collection of three historical narratives in verse and prose authored by different people, recording early conquests of Mahim, the erstwhile island on which Shivaji Park stands. Ruled by Hindu kings in the 12th century, it was conquered by the Gujarat Sultanate in the 14th century and by the Portuguese in the 16th. Some of the oldest families in Shivaji Park trace their roots to the coming of the Hindu kings. The chronicle defines people exclusively by caste. Although that is not my way of thinking, I too have categorized them by caste in the chapter entitled 'Earliest Settlers'. This has been done in the interests of historical truth.

Mahikavatichi Bakhar is as far back temporally as the account goes. Spatially, it is restricted to the area called Dadar, covered by PIN code 400 028. Dadar is the postal district in which Shivaji Park is located. Restricting myself to this PIN code has allowed me to exclude neighbouring areas like Mahim, Matunga West and Prabhadevi into which the story would otherwise have leaked because they fall along a cultural continuum. In describing Dadar too, I have resisted the temptation of including its playhouses, cinema theatres and important cultural centres which have added infinitely to the social life of Shivaji Park residents.

The unique culture of Shivaji Park has arisen from its institutions and the people who came to live here. Some of the most eminent residents of the precinct who have contributed to the growth of this culture are therefore included in the narrative. Also included are efforts made by NGOs and individuals to preserve its character, while the pressure is on to change it radically. What will not change one hopes is the great Arabian Sea beyond and the magnificent trees that offer beauty and shade to walkers in this most democratic of all open spaces in the city.

I must acknowledge with gratitude Amarendra Nandu Dhaneshwar, Anuradha Shah, Shri Ashok Ravat and Shri Govindrao Bhide for the useful conversations I have had with them; Neera Adarkar for sharing with me the Adarkar Associates report that makes a case for Shivaji Park as a heritage precinct; Malini Krishnankutty and Himanshu Burte for pointing me to useful sources of information; my sister Nirmal Limaye for the trouble she took to find me some documents I required; the Dhuru family for giving me books and other documents that I have used liberally in the book; Dr Prasad Modak for giving me time and publications relating to his uncle N.V. Modak; Arun Telang for giving me a copy of Jayant Vitthal Kulkarni's *Shivaji Parkchya Kattyavarun*; Jayant Vitthal Kulkarni for adding me to his mailing list for his recollections about Shivaji Park; Aakash Karkare for sending me a link to the film on Shivaji Park made by his batch of SCMSophia (Social Media Communications Department) students; Sonali Sathaye and Kaustubh Rao for tracking down the name sterculia foetida for me; Ramachandra Guha for permission to use his tribute to Madhu Dandavate in *The Hindu*; Vijaya Rajadhyaksha for permission to use excerpts from the late M.V. Rajadhyaksha's writings; Aniruddha Pendse for permission to use excerpts from the late S.N. Pendse's novel *Kalandar*; Kalpana Swaminathan and Ishrat Syed (Kalpish Ratna) for permission to use an excerpt from their novel *Room 000: Narratives of the Bombay Plague*; Mustansir Dalvi for permission to use excerpts from his blog on Shivaji Park and for taking time to look at and comment on the architectural style of the Mayor's Bungalow; and Swapnil Bhole and Saurab Rao for responding to my SOS and taking photographs to support my text.

1. The Conquest of Mahikavati

'Marching from Daman via Tarapur, Pratap Bimb arrived at Mahikavati, or Mahim.

At the time Mahim was under the rule of Vinaji Ghodel. It took no more than Pratap Bimb's mere presence to drive him away. Pratap Bimb stayed in Mahim for some time to take stock of the place. He saw that the beautiful coastline and the surrounding region, having fallen into the hands of atishudras like Ghodel, who possessed not even a strip of cloth to hide their bottoms, was totally destroyed and desolate. There had been a time, during the reign of the cultured Maratha kings from the Shilahar dynasty, when this region had been bountiful and fertile. Now that it was ill-administered by forest-dwellers like the Pavris, Ghodels, Kolis and Thakers, it had been beggared like an orphan child. It struck Pratap Bimb then, that he could persuade good Brahmin and Maratha people from his own country to settle here and return it to its erstwhile glory.'

—*From* Mahikavatichi Bakhar,
(The Chronicle of Mahikavati), ed. V.K. Rajwade

WRITERS WHO HAVE DESCRIBED THE EVOLUTION OF WHAT used to be seven islands into the city of Bombay/Mumbai have generally limited themselves to the southern islands of Bombay, Mazagaon and Parel where the British and 'native' businessmen lived and worked. Till the early 20th century, the island of Mahikavati, which the British called Mahim, was to them no more than a bit of marshy wasteland, useful only as a place to which unwelcome but necessary businesses like dyeing, liquor distilling and tanning could be pushed. To writers, Dadar—arguably the busiest railway junction in the city—held little interest since it boasted neither of a colonial history nor of grand edifices that spoke of imperial power. Gillian Tindall mentions Dadar three times in *City of Gold.* The first time as the place where, along with Mahim and Parel, the Portuguese had built a huge church; the second time as the Portuguese suburb beyond Parel to which dyers were chased from the Esplanade; and the third time, bracketed with Parel and 'Chichpoogly',* as the thoroughly 'Hindu' suburb through which trains ran.

However, Mahikavati, of which Dadar was a central part, had a fascinating history that pre-dated the arrival of the Portuguese and the British. This history is recorded in *Mahikavatichi Bakhar*. The chronicle itself has a history that stretches back 200 years before it came into the hands of Maharashtra's maverick researcher and historian,

*Present-day Chinchpokli

V.K. Rajwade.* A gentleman named Sadashiv Mahadeo Divekar of Kalyan had acquired it from one Hira Hari Bhandari Sheshvanshi of Vasai. The book Divekar got from Sheshvanshi and handed over to Rajwade had been copied and bound by one Valji Patil Shinde. Rajwade's edition was printed and published by Chitrashala Press of Pune in 1924 CE. It is this edition that has made the chronicle widely available to the public.

Rajwade's arrogant Brahminism displays itself throughout his long, scholarly introduction which is 110 pages to the chronicle's 104. He says of the copy he received, 'So legible and beautifully turned is Valji Patil's handwriting that, had he not appended his name, surname and place of residence to the copy, it would have been impossible to guess that he was not a Brahmin.' Caste and community form the very spine of the Hindu section of the chronicle which comprises six parts. Some parts are in prose, others in verse composed in the ovi metre.** The six parts have been

*Vishwanath Kashinath Rajwade (24 June 1863–31 December 1926), popularly known as Itihasacharya Rajwade, went from village to village in Maharashtra in search of manuscripts, documents and rock edicts and wrote a twenty-two-volume history of the Marathas based on his research.

**An ovi is a four-line poem. The first three lines have the same number of beats and are rhymed. The fourth line is shorter and unrhymed. 'May the blind see the light again / May the sun of righteousness always reign / What is right and good, may people gain / Each and everyone. (An ovi from *Dnyaneshwari*).

written at different times and by different writers between Shaka 1370 and 1500, that is between 1448 and 1578 CE. But they appear to have been put together in book form at least twice previously by anonymous editors before the version that came to Rajwade. This version must have been bound, according to his calculation, 'a hundred and fifty or two hundred years ago'. Since Rajwade's edition was published in 1924, the copy he received may be dated between 1724 and 1774 CE. The first and fourth parts are authored by one Bhagwan Dutt, the sixth by Nayak and Kawale, the second and third by Keshavacharya and the fifth by an anonymous writer. Rajwade gave the six chapters together the title *Mahikavatichi Bakhar* and named the authors as 'Keshavacharya and Others'. Keshavacharya's contribution is about events, battles and the changing fortunes of kings in Mahikavati. The other chapters are chiefly genealogies of those who came with the conquering kings.

In brief then, the story as it has come down to us from the 15th-century chronicle is as follows. It starts in Shaka 1060 (1138 CE), when the whole of south India was ruled by the Kalyani Chalukyas, so named because Kalyani was their capital city. The monarch at the time was Bhulokamalla Chalukya (Someshwar III), who, says the bakhar, was more interested in literary matters than administering his empire. He is best known today as the composer of *Manasollasa*, an encyclopedia of polity, governance, ethics, economics, astronomy, astrology, rhetoric, veterinary medicine, horticulture, perfumes, food, architecture, sports, painting, poetry and music. After India's Independence, Kalyani was renamed Basavakalyan after Basavanna, the founder of a movement for spiritual democracy.

The Kalyani Chalukyas lost power when Basavanna's movement created spiritual turbulence in society. While this was happening in the south, the Anhilpattan Chalukyas in Gujarat were gaining strength. One of their vassals, Raja Govardhan Bimb of Champaner decided to make a foray into Uttar (north) Konkan. The western coastline of India, extending from Gujarat to Goa, was called Konkan. The part that lay directly across from the seven islands that were to form Bombay was referred to as Uttar Konkan. Raja Govardhan Bimb began planning his assault after the commander of his army, Naikrao, and his chief minister Raghunathrao, had declared it feasible and sanctioned it. He chose Rathasaptami which falls in February, as the auspicious day for the attack. It was hoped that by then the 'season of fevers' in north Konkan would have passed. On that happy day, he saw his younger brother Pratap Bimb off on the campaign with ten thousand horsemen.

Here the editor, Rajwade, interrupts the account to alert us to the fact that ten thousand horsemen was not to be understood as that many fighting men. The army itself probably comprised only five thousand men he says, while camp followers, suppliers of provisions and sundry other services made up the rest.

According to the prevailing custom, Govardhan Bimb also sent several administrators and the court priest Hemadpant Chamrey as advisor and counsellor with Pratap Bimb. Amongst them were Keshavrao the army chief, Anandrao, his deputy, Gambhirrao, the army accountant, Purushottamrao, the platoon commander and Balkrishnarao, the chief minister. There was also a treasurer whose name has not been recorded. Four of these men, we are told, were Somvanshi Kshatriyas, one was a Suryavanshi Kshatriya, one a Brahmin and one a Sheshavanshi or Bhandari.

When Pratap Bimb set off on the campaign, he decided not to enter north Konkan via Lat Desh, the old name for south Gujarat. The ruler of Lat Desh did not owe allegiance to Anhilpattan, but to the Barapp Chalukyas and their kin. Barapp Chalukya was hostile to the Anhilpattan Chalukyas. He was on the side of the Kalyani Chalukyas. So, bypassing Lat Desh, Pratap Bimb crossed the Narmada river, the Satpuda mountains and probably took the Ajanta Ghat to reach Paithan. In those days the Narmada, the Satpudas, Ajanta and Paithan were held by chieftains who were hostile to the Kalyani Chalukyas. Moreover the Paithan chieftain, Vikram Bhaum, was connected by marriage to the Champaner Bimbs. When Pratap Bimb reached Paithan, Vikram Bhaum kept him and his entire retinue with him for two years. This was a godsend because, meanwhile, Pratap Bimb had run out of funds. It took two years for his chief minister, Balkrishnarao Somvanshi, to arrange for more.

Once they were in hand, Pratap Bimb and his retinue left Paithan, marched through Nevase and Junnar to reach their destination in north Konkan, comprising today's districts of Ramnagar, Jawhar, Kalyan, Thane and Mumbai. Before he left Paithan, Pratap Bimb was joined by Harbaji Deshmukh. Bimb had not requested him for help. He joined him of his own free will. On the recommendation of Vikram Bhaum, Balaji Shinde, known for his skill in warfare, also joined Pratap Bimb with two thousand horsemen.

Pratap Bimb attacked Daman with this force of 12,000. He cut through the jungles of the Sahyadris to attack Daman first rather than attempt an assault on north Konkan as he had earlier planned, because the capital of north Konkan at the time was the town of Thane, ruled by the Shilahars. Although they had grown weak and could not boast of a single man who had accomplished great feats on the battlefield, some members of the dynasty like Aparaditya and Yeshwantrao still lived in Thane town and district. Amongst them was Vijayaditya Shilahar of Karhad who had many victories to his credit. So, rather than enter the town for a direct encounter with 'this fly in the ointment', Pratap Bimb decided to follow an easier route. He planned to drill a hole in Daman, which lay to the north, test the Thane waters from there and then attack the north Konkan kingdom.

In those days a marauder named Kaloji Siranya had taken over Daman, calling himself the king. After the

Thane Shilahars had lost their might, 'all kinds of scurvy fellows who had been their vassals, had declared themselves kings'. The pretender Kaloji Siranya offered no resistance to Pratap Bimb, surrendering without a fight. Pratap Bimb captured the entire territory from Daman to Chikhli, today's Navsari district. 'Daman town and district are endowed with great natural beauty. To say its beach is breathtaking would be an understatement,' says the writer. 'And yet, this place of sublime beauty had turned into a wilderness under Siranya's chaotic misrule.' In order to rekindle its energy, Pratap Bimb appointed the Kayastha, Harbaji Kulkarni as its administrative head, before marching through Tarapur towards Mahikavati or Mahim. Back then Mahikavati or Mahim referred to Kelwe-Mahim on the mainland. The name was later transferred to Mahim island.

Mahim was ruled by Vinaji Ghodel as the excerpt at the head of this chapter tells us. We also know that Pratap Bimb's mere presence was enough to make him flee. Bimb thought the only way the region could be restored to its erstwhile beauty was by encouraging reputed Marathas and Brahmins from his own country to settle down in the district.

Pratap Bimb sent Balkrishnarao Somvanshi from Mahim to take over the entire region up to Walukeshwar. Along the way, he encountered Yeshwantrao Shilahar, the king of Thane-Konkan, and killed him in battle. It transpired that Yeshwantrao had overcome Aparaditya Shilahar to grab the Thane seat. 'So insignificant was Yeshwantrao as a ruler,' says Rajwade, that not a single rock inscription or copperplate exists from his time. A large part of the south of north Konkan had been captured by the Kadamb of Goa although he was barely managing to subsist on the handful of villages he still ruled. He too fell to Balkrishnarao's sword. After killing him, Balkrishnarao arrived in Kalwa which was under the rule of an inconsequential Maratha called Kokatya, possibly a contemptuous form of Kokate. The man surrendered without a fight. From Kalwa, Somvanshi marched to Madh on the sea coast, and from there directly to Walukeshwar via Vesave, Juhu, Vahinale and Rajanphar. He saw the sacred Banganga and the idol of Hanumant and rested beside the sea for five days.

Rajwade surmises that, since his army was with him, Balkrishnarao must have camped in the open space that adjoined Banganga where the Government House stood in Rajwade's time. Balkrishnarao calculated that the distance between Daman and Walukeshwar, taking Kelwe-Mahim on the mainland as the central point, would have been 28 kos which translates into 84 miles. Says Rajwade, 'It would not be wrong to call Pratap Bimb's kingdom the Kingdom of Mahikavati or Mahim with its capital at Kelwe-Mahim.' So lacking in inhabitants was this territory, that no Brahmin was available to consecrate Pratap Bimb's kingdom and to bless him. It was only when he sent for purohits, shastris and pandits from Paithan that these rituals could be conducted with the pomp and ceremony that were his due. Meanwhile, he had written to Govardhan Bimb in Champaner asking him to send his son Mahi and as many residents of Champaner as possible to settle in the new kingdom. Accordingly Mahi Bimb arrived in Kelwe-Mahim with sixty-six high-caste families from Champaner. Other lesser families also followed. Among the sixty-six families, the notable ones were twenty-seven Somvanshis, twelve Suryavanshis and nine Sheshvanshis. The rest were Panchals, Kunbis and Agris. In this way Pratap Bimb brought a dead place to life. Soon trade, industry, religion and culture began to flourish there.

The reign of the Bimbs lasted for one hundred years till Shaka 1163 (1241 CE). One may say this was one of the first of many migrations into Bombay where the settlers had nothing but contempt for the 'natives', in this case mainland adivasis and island fishermen.

During Pratap Bimb's reign, a member of the Shilahar dynasty put an army together, confined Pratap Bimb to Sashti island (Salsette) and took back the old Shilahar capital of Thane. As a result, Pratap Bimb who had established his capital in nearby Kelwe-Mahim lost all the territory that lay to the north of Thane creek, including Vasai, Sopara, Kelwe-Mahim, Tarapur, Dahanu and Daman. He was left with ten groups of villages, extending from Ghodbunder to Walukeshwar to the south of the creek, which he handed over to the care of havaldars. Having lost Kelwe-Mahim,

Pratap Bimb moved to the south of Vandre (Bandra) and made Mahim as we know it today, his capital. This is the Mahim island where Dadar evolved in the 1920s. Later, one of the largest open spaces in the city of Mumbai, Shivaji Park, was created in the western part of Dadar. Although Dadar is not mentioned in *Mahikavatichi Bakhar* along with Juhu and Vandre, it existed as we shall soon see.

The later history of Mahim belongs to other conquerors, including the Portuguese. But none of them altered the looks, demography or occupations of the people during the four hundred years that followed Pratap Bimb's rule. The Portuguese were interested only in trade and converting the local people to Christianity. Both these aims thrived, the latter to the extent that they built Our Lady of Salvation Church that still stands in Dadar in its fourth avatar.

Arvind Rane, a member of the Adishakti Laboratory for Theatre Art Research, Pondicherry, traces his roots to Raja Bimb. He narrates an amusing community legend about the Raja's contribution to Mumbai's crime scene. When Bimbaraja had a 'problem' with somebody, he would invite the local chieftains and warriors to a feast. He would give them an idea of his problem and place a supari before them. Whoever picked it up would be responsible for eliminating the problem. That, says Rane, is the origin of the phrase 'giving supari' used by Mumbai's underworld for contract killings.

2. Dadar

'This story belongs to the time when Lady Jamshedji Road in Dadar had begun to shed its old skin rapidly. Back then there used to be just a few scattered buildings around the station. A treeless plot of land, which turned into a pond in the rains, lay opposite Chhabildas School. In the summer, local boys played cricket there. Tilak Bridge had been completed only a few years before; but many years would pass before it became crowded with traffic. Kohinoor Cinema was still a couple of years away. At present there was a yarn-dyeing factory on the plot; and the air rang all day with the thump-thump-thump of wooden batons beating the yarn.

'One day the factory was razed. The buildings and dilapidated chawls in the vicinity were demolished. The well was filled up. A pond that had nudged its way in between the buildings was filled. The Dadar English School shifted house to the Popatlal Chawl nearby. And Kohinoor Cinema rose where all these places had been. Suddenly the area was bright with lights. One life was ending and another pulsating into being.'

—Opening passage from Kalandar,
Shri Na Pendse

'Other than a couple of roads, the entire strip from Dadar to Mahim was covered extensively with wadis. Tall palm trees grew with seasonal vegetables planted at their base. A few huts were scattered here and there with, occasionally, a larger cottage. Very rarely did you see a well-appointed bungalow belonging to a comparatively well-to-do resident. Pathways seemingly made to mislead the newcomer twisted and turned through the wadis. A couple of them still exist like museum exhibits. Larger alleys wove untidily, drunkenly, along the sides of homes and embankments, narrow in some parts, broad in others for no apparent reason. They turned to mud in the monsoon and to dust for the rest of the year, and were alive for all twelve months with smells of diverse kinds. Many of those alleys later turned into neat roads. Indeed, if you were to look up the ancestry of some of the majestic roads of Shivaji Park, you would find it in these alleys. … Take the expansive Gokhale Road, for instance, now flanked by elegant buildings. Thirty-five years ago, it did not exist, not even as a muddy track. It bulldozed its way into existence through trees, lush vegetation and huts. And the splendid, much talked-about Shivaji Park, that gift to lovers, that expansive maidan which lends itself to cricket matches, cultural festivals and political rallies attended by lakhs, surrounded by those neat habitations, that too rose on land where once palm groves, vegetable patches and huts had stood. Before the park was created, we children felt delicious tremors of adventure when we crossed those parts to reach the beach. We looked around in fear, happy for each other's company, as we walked the stretch to the beach. The Dadar Chowpatty, as it later came to be known, had very few visitors then. The

silence that wrapped it was a perfect match for the crematorium that stood beside it.

Tilak Bridge, as we gathered from what adults said, was something of an engineering wonder. When the gigantic hulk was taking shape, we hung around it, mouths agape. When it was half built we capered around on it... I recall distinctly the time when a friend challenged me to a race up the bridge. I was game. Off we went running madly till suddenly, the bridge ended. We had forgotten that it was only half complete. We were fortunate to have feet with efficient brakes, or else...'

—Old Picture, *excerpted from* Nivadlele Kharde, *M.V. Rajadhyaksha*

The Lady Jamshedji Road that Pendse refers to extended all the way to Kabutarkhana, or pigeon home, in those days. The southern section was in Dadar, the northern in Mahim. The Dadar section was later renamed N.C. Kelkar Road. The road served as an approach to Mahim Causeway, which was built in 1845. Getting to Bandra from Mahim then used to be a very dangerous undertaking, especially in the monsoon. The only transport available to cross Mahim creek was a ferry service. The hazards of the crossing became tragically clear when, within the single year 1841, some twenty boats capsized, killing dozens of people. The British government had for long been trying to raise funds for a causeway through public subscription, and failed. The 1841 tragedy so grieved Lady Avabai Jamsetjee, wife of Sir Jamsetjee Jeejeebhoy, Baronet, that she made a generous offer of Rs 1,00,000 for the causeway, topping it up with another Rs 40,000 when the estimated costs escalated. The offer came with the proviso that citizens would not be charged a toll. The final cost of the causeway amounted to Rs 1,57,000; but since Lady Jamsetjee had paid the major part of it, the road leading to it was named after her.

Lady Jamshedji Road, which forms the eastern boundary of Shivaji Park, has been strangely divided by the postal authorities. The pin code for the park side of the road is 400 028, which is Dadar. The opposite side of the same road is 400 016, which is Mahim. This story is about Dadar. So it will not cross the road to Mahim.

It is a matter of speculation how Dadar came by its name. The place, or at least a part of it, appears to have been known as Salvasong during Portuguese times. The British called it Lower Mahim. Either way it held little importance in the colonial scheme of things. The Portuguese, who were interested only in trade and Christianity, did well on both counts elsewhere along the coast, for instance in Goa. But in Salvasong they did well only on one count, Christianity. They harvested thousands of souls for whose upward journey they built Our Lady of Salvation Church, later to be known as Portuguese Church, at the south end of Dadar. The East India Company men were in India for trade, not conversions. They left Dadar strictly alone, fully expecting it always to remain a district of swamps, coconut groves, paddy fields and vegetables gardens. If they built roads and railways that passed through Dadar, it was only to improve their trading prospects further afield. However, as a spinoff, Dadar became an attractive place for 'natives' to live in. The first trickle began soon after 1867 when the local line between Churchgate and Virar, passing through Dadar, was inaugurated. By the first decade of the 20th century, the trickle had turned into a regular stream.

One theory says Dadar was named after the station. Dadar means stairs in Marathi. Some local people recall that a wooden bridge in the area gave the station its name. That 'wooden bridge' could have been the small stairway that is known to have spanned the Flats between Mahim and Parel islands. When the British built the railways, they named the station serving Mahim island Dadar, because it was located near the stairway. In time the areas to the east and west of the station took its name. This sounds like a plausible theory. Other locals believe that the area was called Dadar first, and the station was named after it. They recall their fathers and grandfathers telling them that they used to cross over from one wadi to the next over improvised wooden ladders, dadars, placed over low-lying areas for the purpose. Since this part of Mahim island was full of wadis and low-lying areas, the whole place assumed the nature of a stairway—dadar. This too sounds plausible.

Another theory comes from Samuel Townsend Sheppard. In his book *Bombay Place-Names and Street-Names* (1917), he points out that Kolis used the word 'dadar' for any locality that lay on the outskirts of a village. As analogy, he gives the example of another place called Dadar which was located on the outskirts of Kelwe village in Thane district. If that was the case, outside which village on Mahim island did our Dadar lie? Sheppard does not say. Perhaps he could not say because no villages existed on Mahim island as far as we can tell. They did exist in Girgaum, Mazagaon, Andheri, Bandra and Chembur, and still do as gaothans. But there is not a single gaothan on Mahim island. However, there is a Mahim Koliwada, a colony of fishermen. Could this be properly called a village? And if so, could Dadar have been seen as lying on its southern outskirts?

Finally, in his thesis *Recognizing and Preserving the Historic Identity of Dadar West, Bombay*, Vineet Shrikant Date refers to another theory which holds that Dadar was named so because it stood on higher ground than the surrounding areas, becoming in effect a stairway. As a former resident of the area, he supports the theory because he does not remember Dadar ever getting flooded, not even in torrential rains. But then I, as a longtime resident of the area, have memories of wading through knee-high water to my office in Worli during torrential rains. In any case, can one imagine the kolis and wadi owners of old standing on this high ground and thinking metaphorically that it was a stairway, and calling it Dadar?

Whatever the origin of the name, we must now turn to Dadar and its landmarks which continue to contribute to the socio-cultural life of Shivaji Park. In his novel *Kalandar*, set in the Dadar-Shivaji Park area, Shri Na Pendse describes the house where his protagonist lived as standing across from 'the extensive coconut grove that lay behind Da Silva school'. The novel is set in the early 1930s. Dr Antonio da Silva High School was founded eight decades earlier in 1851, by Rev. John Braz Fernandes, Vicar of the Church of Our Lady of Salvation, and Dr Antonio da Silva, a local landowner. It was known as St John's School till 1875. After Dr da Silva donated a large part of his estate to it, it was renamed Dr Antonio da Silva High School. The sweeping building with a pitched roof that was constructed then in the extensive da Silva Wadi, still stands as a proud piece of Dadar heritage, although surrounded now not by trees, but by the ugly conglomerations of a carelessly growing metropolis.

The school acquired another kind of historical significance when the city's seventh milestone was discovered outside its southern wall, opposite the Kabutarkhana. Altogether sixteen such milestones have been discovered and listed by the Mumbai Metropolitan Regional Development Authority's Heritage Committee. Some were half buried under repaired pavements and widened roads. The inscription on the 4-foot high basalt stones, erected between 1816 and 1837, told horse-carriage drivers how many miles they were from St Thomas's Cathedral in Fort, designated the city's centre. The stone outside da Silva school reads: 'VII miles from St Thomas Cathedral'.

In the coordinated Mumbai bombings that occurred between 6.54 and 7.06 p.m. on 13 July 2011, the first bomb exploded at Opera House and the second at Zaveri Bazaar. The third, which exploded at 7.06 p.m., had been placed on an electric pole at the bus stop outside the school near Kabutarkhana. Fortunately, the school had given over for the day and no schoolchild figured among the twenty-six killed and 130 injured in the bombings.

A landmark that came up half-a-century after Dr Antonio da Silva High School was the Dadar Sarvajanik Vachanalaya (Dadar Public Library). Its history bears witness to times when books were considered vital to people's growth. The library was started in a very small way by a like-minded group of individuals led by Mahadev Ganesh Gore, a voracious reader. Housed at first in the Shri Ram Mandir on Bhavani Shankar Road where Dadar's central post office stands, the library, comprising chiefly Mr Gore's private collection stored in a large tin trunk, was inaugurated on 23 August 1907. In the following January, it was shifted to the more spacious home of G.N. Akshikar, the founder of Chhabildas High School, then known as Dadar English School. Soon it outgrew Mr Akshikar's home. After several moves, Mr Kashinath Devji Dhuru, the second president of the library, who will figure prominently in a later chapter, helped to find it a place in a new building that had come up in the Chhabildas Lane. In 1926, the municipality bought some land nearby to sell as building plots. The library bought a plot for itself and within a few years moved into its own rightful space. The narrow lane in which this building stands is named Vachanalaya Marg after the library. Its subscription fees still remain incredibly low, but it makes a little more money by renting out an assembly hall that Kashinath Dhuru built above the library. Known as Dhuru Hall, it was initially meant for Union meetings, but was renovated in the '60s and thrown open for more general use. The library celebrated its 100th anniversary in an unusual manner. It commissioned writers to contribute well-researched articles on diverse aspects of Dadar, its history, its places and its people. The collection was put together in a book entitled *Bahurangi Bahudhangi Dadar* (Dadar of Many Ways and Many Colours). It has become a useful handbook for journalists and local historians and has been a valuable resource for the present project.

As Dadar's population increased, the ponds and tanks that once dotted the landscape, were filled up, often giving their names to the roads built on the reclaimed land. During Mumbai's plague years (1896–1914), the municipality passed a law which also made it compulsory for these water bodies to be filled up. Hansali tank, which stood at the southernmost end of N.C. Kelkar Road where it meets Tilak Bridge, has become a garden, named Veer

Kotwal Udyan after Vithal Laxman Kotwal, a reformer and revolutionary. The garden once occupied a much larger area than it does today and was called Kale Maidan, or Black Park because the coke from a nearby textile mill that had been used to fill up the tank had made the park black. Kale Maidan's proximity to Dadar station made it a convenient spot for farmers travelling from Salsette and Bassein to sell their farm and other produce here. When the maidan shrank to a smaller garden dense with trees, the farmers shifted their market to the Tilak Bridge pavement across the road a little way up from V. Shantaram's Plaza cinema. In time, the farmers were replaced by wholesale merchants. But the location and timings of the market have remained unchanged over the decades. Business still starts at five in the morning and ends at nine, leaving behind no sign of the hectic buying, selling and haggling that has gone on before.

At the south end of N.C. Kelkar Road stands the elaborately designed and decorated Jain Mandir built in 1905. Across from there is Kirtikar Market, where, even today you can buy almost anything from pin to pestle. In the old days, bullock carts and handcarts transporting grain would park in the square between mandir and the market. Here the produce was off-loaded and carried to the market. Hundreds of pigeons would flap around to pick up grain spilt from the sacks. When trucks took over some of the transport business, pigeons, busy gobbling grain, would get crushed under their wheels. This saddened the Muni at the Jain Mandir. According to Vikas Patil, a contributor to *Bahudhangi Bahurangi Dadar*, the Muni consulted a nearby shopkeeper, Vallabhji Ratansi Vora, to find a way out of this daily massacre. Sometime in 1936, Vora succeeded in persuading the municipal corporation to allow the centre of the square to be turned into a kabutarkhana, a home for pigeons. Permission was granted and a circular area in the square was fenced off with iron railings where pigeons could be fed grain. Vora also set up the Dadar Kabutar Khana Trust, which constructed roosts and birdbaths for the pigeons. Kabutarkhana has since been declared a heritage space.

Blogger Rudolph Furtado adds interesting details to the story. The grain that devotees visiting the Jain temple feed to the pigeons as their religious duty, is not sufficient for them. So the Trust sources funds from wholesalers in other markets to make up their daily requirement. Medical services are on the house. Vets from the veterinary college in Parel make regular visits to Kabutarkhana, diluting multivitamins into the pigeons' drinking water to strengthen their immunity against disease.

Cross the road from Kirtikar Market and you are at the entrance of the Dadar Departmental Stores which has been around, as far as I know, from the late 1940s. I bought my first badminton racquet there and my mother our ironing board. We have bought irons and light fittings there, folding tables, chairs, alarm clocks and almost anything we needed for the house that was not high-end but comfortably middle-class. The multi-purpose store was burnt to ashes in an all-consuming conflagration in 1994; but, like the phoenix, it rose from the ashes as the structure that stands there now.

Swapnil Bhole

Dadar kabutarkhana with the Jain Mandir in the background

The Kabutarkhana square is as crowded with pigeons as with people and traffic, making it one of the busiest squares in Dadar. Besides the general public, there is a constant stream of devotees to various places of worship in this syncretic space. There is a Maruti Mandir in front of the Jain Mandir which used to be known as the Police Maruti temple because a small police chowki stood nearby. Later it came to be called Puratan Vatvruksha Hanuman Mandir or the Ancient Banyan Tree Hanuman Temple because it had once been a small shrine under an ancient banyan tree.

Diagonally across from the Jain temple stands the Peer Baghdadi Darga and Mosque, built with public donations in memory of Syed Fatehali Afabdi, known as Peer Baghdadi. He passed away on 14 July 1888. The plot where the mosque stands had been bought by his disciples twenty years earlier. The dargah and mosque were constructed after he passed away. The Ramzan Iftari held here is said to be the biggest in Mumbai.

Dadar, served by both railways, Central and Western, has become a hub for many kinds of business. Horticulturists from the city's hinterland have converted a lane that runs parallel to the railway line into the city's biggest wholesale flower market. Popularly known as Phool Galli, you smell it well before you see it. The rains make it unwalkably slushy. But go there between October and May early in the morning when the tempos have been and gone, and your eyes can feast on every hue and colour under the sun. Roses, gerberas, orchids, carnations and the stunningly beautiful birds of paradise command your attention first. Desi flowers like mogra, bakul, rajnigandha, sevanti and chafa sold from baskets may not stun the eyes, nor make it to elegant vases in well-appointed homes; but they scent the air with their heady fragrances and are strung lovingly, romantically, around glossy buns and braids. Whether you live in Colaba or Malabar Hill, Sion or Dharavi, the gerberas and orchids in your vases or the mogras in your hair come from Dadar Phool Galli.

Swapnil Bhole

Dadar Phool Galli

Even before shops and markets came up in Dadar offering employment to tradespeople, carpenters, weavers and ironsmiths, the major employer of unskilled labour were the mills. The first to be built was the Bombay Spinning and Weaving Company in 1856, located in Tardeo. By 1900, the number had increased to 136. Scattered from Byculla to Dadar, they began with 6,500 workers. By 1980 the workers numbered something like 3,00,000. While the mill-owners included, along with Parsis, Gujaratis and Marwaris, the Baghdadi Jewish family of David Sassoon, the labour was provided mainly by Kolis, but also by

Bhandaris and Kunbis and, most importantly, by the castes known as untouchables. Inhumanly discriminated against in Maharashtra's rural hinterland, they found a space in Bombay's mills that they could claim as their own. The mill-workers gave birth to a vibrant culture of music and drama, acquiring a fearless political voice, which writers like Annabhau Sathe, Baburao Bagul, Shankarrao Kharat and Narayan Surve used forcefully in their poetry and fiction.

The mill-owners housed their workers in chawls: dingy one-room tenements without light or air. In his book, *Mills for Sale: The Way Ahead*, Darryl D'Monte cites a comment made in 1929 about a chawl in Dadar as being a dark, unwholesome den 'which of necessity breeds disease and pestilence'. To live and work in Girangaon (The Village of Mills)—as the mill district came to be called in contrast to Girgaum, where more habitable chawls were built for upper-caste, white-collar workers—was no dream come true. Workers lived ten to a room. The shift system in mills ensured that one lot had just enough place to sleep while the other went to work. But this subhuman-level existence helped the workers send money home. The Konkan and the Desh (the plateau region) lived off a money-order economy. So when the big textile mill strike of 1982 led to mills being closed one by one and mill-owners selling vast acres of mill land for enormous sums of money, the workers and their families hit rock bottom. The unique culture they had bred withered away and died. Sudhir Patwardhan has caught this transformation in his large painting *Lower Parel*; Ramu Ramanathan in his play *Cotton 56 Polyester 84* directed by Sunil Shanbag; and Mahesh Manjrekar in his film *City of Gold* based on Jayant Pawar's play *Adhantar*.

Narayan Surve, who worked for a few years in Dadar's Kohinoor Mill No. 3, begins his 'Mumbaichi Lavni' (Love Song for Mumbai) with the lines 'It is seven in the morning and the siren sings / In right high style the first shift begins / The wheels go round, the yarn spills out / We dress the earth with the sweat of our brow.'

As children, we woke up to the sound of the siren. The Kohinoor Mill stood on 4.9 acres of land at the junction of Lady Jamshedji Road, Gokhale Road, Dadasaheb Rege Marg and the short road that leads to Shivaji Park. This crossroads is now known as Shiv Sena Bhavan junction. The old mill decayed bit by bit after it locked its great gates for all time. First the siren stopped hooting. Then the mill structure sprang cracks. Then grass grew in the cracks. On 21 July 2005, the land was sold as a single parcel for Rs 421 crore to a joint venture floated by Unmesh, son of former Lok Sabha Speaker Manohar Joshi, and Raj Thackeray who was still with the Sena then. Thackeray offloaded his share four years later at a profit which was publicly declared as Rs 62 crore, but privately rumoured to be Rs 300 crore. His decision had much to do with the economic crash of 2008. The remaining partners built a fifty-two-storey, 203-metre-high multi-purpose tower, Kohinoor Square, on the plot. The builders claimed it was the tallest structure in India. I do not know about India, but in Shivaji Park it is tall enough to get into your eyes wherever you are.

There used to be another mill in Dadar that added its siren to the Kohinoor Mill wail. It stood on the other side of Dadar, on what was then called Cadell Road and renamed later as Swatantrya Veer Savarkar Marg. The mill was established in 1890 by Jacob Sassoon, grandson of the great industrialist David Sassoon. The family used to be known for their philanthropy as the Rothschilds of the East. Jacob named the mill E.D. Sassoon Mill after his father Elias David. He sold the mill during the great depression of the 1930s and moved to Shanghai where the family had business interests. He was driven out from there by the Japanese during World War II and returned to Bombay, occupying his old cottage at the far end of the mill precincts overlooking the sea. It was a typical vernacular-style cottage with verandas back and front and a pitched, tiled roof. The mill was later taken over by the government-owned National Textile Corporation and renamed India United Mill No. 6, Indu Mills for short. The mill closed down in 2011, and the land was handed over to the state government in 2014 for a memorial to Dr B.R. Ambedkar, the father of the Indian Constitution. The cost of the memorial spread over 12 acres of the mill land is estimated at Rs 766 crore. It will have a 351-foot tall statue of Dr Ambedkar and a 2.5 km walkway that will take his followers to the feet of the statue. The memorial will also be linked to the nearby Chaitya Bhoomi where Dr Ambedkar's ashes are kept; making it easy for the lakhs who visit it on 6 December, his death anniversary, to pay their respects.

If the war undermined the Sassoon family's fortunes, it provided business for one Mr Khandke, a tailor by birth who was contracted to make uniforms for the British army. So sizeable was the order, that he built eleven chawls on its back. The Khandke building on R.K. Vaidya Marg off Ranade Road is where Bal Thackeray grew up. His father Keshav Sitaram Thackeray began celebrating the Navratri festival in this building to cock a snook, so to say, at Brahmins who had monopolized the Ganapati festival. Perhaps it was in response to his rebellion that the Ganapati festival became the mass celebration it is today.

Over time, many chawl dwellers have sold their rooms to chartered accountants, advocates, astrologers and doctors for office and clinic space. The old dingy rooms have been painted and fitted with glass doors and air conditioners. But many of these cosmetically treated structures are over 100 years old and, although built to last, are now likely candidates for redevelopment. To carry forward Shri Na Pendse's metaphor, Dadar along with Shivaji Park is shedding its skin yet again. The changes we are seeing are as dramatic as the ones he and M.V. Rajadhyaksha saw in the early 1930s. The most important change is in the skyline and in the growing loss of a sense of community.

3. The Earliest Settlers

Once upon a time eons ago, there was a daitya named Tilakasur who had grown very arrogant. So Lord Shiva tied him to an oil-mill and said to Nandi, 'Now turn the mill and wring this daitya into a twist.' While Nandi was doing Shiva's bidding, Shiva felt unaccountably exhausted. A drop of sweat fell from his divine brow onto the earth. From that drop sprang a man who instantly broke into a song praising Shiva. Highly pleased with him, Shiva said, 'I shall name you Bhavgun because you are singing my praises.' Then he added, 'I am very thirsty. You must fetch me some water.' Bhavgun looked around. He saw no water. 'Where can I fetch water from, my Lord, for I see none,' he said. Then Lord Shiva created a palm tree at the top of which hung clusters of sweet fruit. Bhavgun climbed the tree at once and fetched down a cluster. Cracking one fruit open, he offered it to the Lord to drink from. Pleased with Bhavgun, Lord Shiva said, 'I hereby appoint you the keeper of Kubera's treasury.'

—Origin myth of Bhandaris

THE MARATHI WORD BHANDAR MEANS TREASURE-HOUSE. The keeper of a treasure-house is a bhandari. There is room to suspect that the elders of the Bhandari community created the myth of their origin after the event, so to say, seeing as it covers the two professions that they took to when circumstances prevented them from practising the one they were born to as Kshatriyas—fighting wars. When the Hindu kings of Mahikavati had fought and won their wars, they appointed Bhandaris as keepers of their treasuries. When the Portuguese conquered Mahikavati, the Bhandaris became toddy-tappers. The myth of their origin was probably thought up to inject some glory into these enforced occupations.

There is an argument, however, that Bhandaris were originally not Kshatriyas at all, but Kolis. That is why many returned to fishing when royal treasuries became a thing of the past. Some of them began to make toddy later, when the East India Company men discovered the alcoholic drink and found much solace in it. Gillian Tindall tells us that Gerald Aungier, the second governor of Bombay (1669–77), 'openly disapproved of the drinking habits he found among the Europeans of the colony; in particular, he disapproved of those who partook of the local toddy, or of the mixture of this with lime juice, plain water, rosewater and sugar that composed the accursed Bombay punch, the shame, scandal and ruin of religion.'

What lends credence to the claim that the Bhandaris

were a sub-caste of Kshatriyas, however, is the use they were put to by Gerald Aungier. On taking over as governor and keen to find a way to bring a semblance of order into this wildly chaotic place called Bombay, he recruited Bhandari youth to form a Bhandari Militia. The militia was chiefly created to deal with street gangs that robbed sailors. Clearly Aungier had gathered that Bhandaris were known to be fighters. Even today, it is not by accident that an overwhelming number of them join the police force.

Historically, Bhandaris were not territorial soldiers like Suryavanshi Kshatriyas. Their expertise lay on the high seas. They were reputed to have been sent by Chandragupta Maurya to take charge of the sea trade that flourished off the west coast of the country. Back then, the largest and busiest sea port was Nala Sopara, now rather an insignificant part of Greater Mumbai. Bhandaris still form a large part of the population here. Mumbai saw their numbers on 17 August 2018, when they marched in protest against the arrest of one of their own, Vaibhav Raut, as a terror-plot suspect.

The real pride of Bhandaris is their ancestor Kanhoji Angre (1669–1729) who was appointed admiral of Shivaji's fleet. He was regarded as a terror by the British and was invincible at sea. No enemy had been able to conquer his chief base, the Vijaydurg fort. Known as the 'Eastern Gibraltar', its unique location made it impregnable. Between 1702 and 1729, Angre fought fourteen battles against the Siddis, the Portuguese and British merchant ships, winning them all. When the British fleet reached Bombay in 1721 and attacked Angre's outpost Alibag jointly with the Portuguese, they suffered a rout. In 1724, the Portuguese felt compelled to sign a pact with the Marathas. In the same year the Dutch attacked Vijaydurg and were chased away. It is not surprising that Bhandaris should hold up Angre as an icon of their past valour.

The community's website flaunts a list of other Bhandari luminaries, many of them associated with art, music and the film industry. The list ends with cricket: 'Go to Shivaji Park today and you will find—except for one or two—all the nets belong to the Bhandari community members. … The King Maker Dronacharya Acharekar the man whom Sachin Tendulkar owes his cricketing skills to, belongs to this community.'

Achrekar, who founded the Kamath Memorial Cricket Club at Shivaji Park, where he coached and nurtured Test players Sachin Tendulkar, Ajit Agarkar, Chandrakant Pandit, Vinod Kambli and Pravin Amre, passed away on 2 January 2019 at his Shivaji Park home. 'Achrekar sir taught us the virtues of playing straight and living straight,' said Tendulkar at his funeral. Sharadashram Vidyamandir in Dadar where he, Kambli and Agarkar schooled, has become a Mecca for young cricketing aspirants. They come from all over the country in the hope that the school which brought international fame to the trio might do the same for them.

Later in this narrative, I will have occasion to mention

two other names from the Bhandari community—Pandit Sharadchandra Arolkar, the reclusive vocalist of the Gwalior Gharana who lived and died in Shivaji Park, and sculptor N.G. Pansare, who created the equestrian statue of Shivaji that stands on the westernside of the park.

Another community that came with the Hindu kings and settled first in Thane district and later migrated to Worli, Prabhadevi, Dadar and Mahim, were the Suryavanshi Kshatriyas. Among them were the Dhurus, Kavlis, Churis, Kores, Vaidyas, Patils and Thakurs. Here is the story of one family, the Dhurus of Dhuru Lodge on Veer Savarkar Marg, whose 18th-century migration has been chronicled by a member of the family, Vasumati Dhuru, in her book *Prapitamah Kashinath Devji Dhuru ani Suryavanshi Kshatriya Dnyati Samaj* (Great Grandfather Kashinath Devji Dhuru and the Suryavanshi Kshatriya Community, Granthali 2014).

'It was around 1760. The place was Edvan in Kelwe-Mahim, Palghar Taluka, District Thane. The bullock carts which had left Edvan in the morning reached Thane at lunchtime. …The caravan was made up of ten or fifteen families. The country was overrun by thugs. To travel in ones and twos was dangerous, particularly with women. The paths ran through jungles. Tigers and other wild beasts prowled around. That is why the entire clan of uncles and nephews had decided to leave Edvan together. But who were these people? Why were they leaving Edvan to settle in Bombay? ... Perhaps they were looking for greener pastures or perhaps they were fired by the spirit of adventure. They were already familiar with Bombay. It had been their market. A daily launch service carried the men and their produce of rice, coconuts and dried fish from Thane to Bombay. The word 'daily' for the ferry had entered the common vocabulary. Perhaps they felt it would make more sense to do business from the Worli-Prabhadevi-Mahim belt instead.

'When the bullock carts reached Worli-Prabhadevi, the women jumped out, tucked their pallus in and got down to work. The children were excited to find that, like Edvan, this place too was dense with coconut palms, toddy palms, mango, jackfruit and bakul trees. The leader of the clan was Beduji Gomji Dhuru. His wife Kamlabai was thrilled. "Oh my," she exclaimed. "I've just counted forty-seven coconut trees. Are they all ours?" Beduji replied proudly, "Why do you think I made all those trips by launch? It was to choose the best place I could find. I came home only after I had sealed the deal."'

Vasumati Dhuru admits that when she decided to write about her illustrious ancestor Kashinath Devji Dhuru, she had not realized that no documents of the family's early history existed. For example, no details of Beduji Gomji Dhuru's land transaction were available. Much of Dhuru's story is based on family lore. As far as the land transaction goes, it is possible that no documents were made. The18th-century history of the islands is full of the Portuguese, Marathas, Mughals and the British fighting for control. In these unstable conditions, ownership of land was of least concern to the Company. Again, many conquering powers from Bimb Raja to the Portuguese had given away land as inam, or reward, for services rendered. In *Mumbaiche Varnan* (Mumbai Described, 1863), Govind Narayan Madgavkar cites a chronicle that was in the possession of an early Pathare Prabhu settler, which recorded the gifting of the whole of Worli village as inam. It is therefore likely that the land Beduji Gomji Dhuru bought was a private, undocumented transaction. The Company men left the locals free to enter into land transactions. The greater the number of people who settled along Bombay's western coast, the safer the harbours would be. Land was not expensive either. So the families that came from Edvan bought as much as they could afford. Soon their properties came to be known by their owners' names—Dhuru Wadi, Kavli Wadi, Churi Wadi, Patil Wadi and Kore Wadi among others. Located on the other side of Dadar are wadis belonging to East Indians—Fernandes Wadi, Gomes Wadi, etc.

When the Dhuru family first came to Dadar, they built themselves a large cottage like the one they had owned in Edvan. It had verandas back and front, family rooms in the middle and a pitched, tiled roof on top. When the family began to prosper, Beduji's grandson Laxmanji told his son Keshav that it was now time for them to build a bungalow that would match Bombay's high style and the bungalows that Muslims and Parsis had built in upper Mahim. Soon the new bungalow was built. This is the bungalow in which Beduji's great-great-great-grandson, Kashinath Devji Dhuru, was born on 19 July 1849. And this is the bungalow—Dhuru Lodge on Veer Savarkar Marg—in which Kashinathji's great-grandchildren and great-great-grandchildren live today.

The surroundings of Dhuru Lodge were known as Mahim Woods when Kashinath Dhuru was growing up. There were no railways, no roads and no schools on the island. The young boy schooled under arduous conditions. He had to walk to his primary school in Worli; then to his secondary English school in Parel; then to Robert Money Mission School in Grant Road; and finally to the General Assembly Mission School in Kalbadevi from where he matriculated. Matriculation was considered a good qualification for a job in those days. He got a job in the Water Works department of the municipality where he served for the next thirty-nine years. He rose rapidly from 'correspondence clerk' on Rs 30 per month to 'assistant to the special engineer' on Rs 300 a month. The Tulsi and Tansa lake schemes, which brought water to a thirsty Bombay, were the most important projects he worked on in his four-decade career. When he retired, he was granted the municipality's 'good service pension' whereby a Rs 50 bonus was added to the regular half salary that pensioners received. He was also appointed Justice of the Peace.

Kashinathji was a progressive man who believed in women's education. Vasumati Dhuru tells us of a daughter-in-law of the family, married at the age of twelve or thirteen, who had no education at all. This was unacceptable to Kashinathji. Since there was no school for girls in Dadar, he enrolled her in the well-known Chandaramji Girls School at Charni Road. Now, unlike his times, there were trains. So the young girl would ride to Dadar station in the family's horse-drawn carriage, accompanied by an old retainer. The carriage would return to pick her up from the station. The girl was the only married 'woman' in her class. She went to school dressed in a nine-yard sari, wearing all the gold ornaments she was supposed to wear as the daughter-in-law of a respectable family.

Kashinathji was a philanthropist who took a leading part in Dadar's civic life. I reproduce below a translation of the letter Dr B.R. Ambedkar wrote to him on 9 October 1927:

Samaj Samata Sangh (Social Equality League)
To Shri Kashinathji Dhuru, Dadar.

I have heard from a reliable source that you plan to spend a large sum of money on building a public assembly hall in Dadar. I have also heard that it is your noble idea to throw the hall open, in the interests of the country and its unity, to all organizations, whatever the religion or ideology they represent. If this worthy aim is indeed true, we, the Samaj Samata Sangh, being founded on similar principles, would like to present our justified claim to the hall. You will see the truth of our claim when you read the enclosed note about the organization. It would give us great satisfaction to meet you in this regard at any time that you may be pleased to appoint.

Yours humbly,
Bhimrao Ambedkar

Ajit, Kashinathji's great-great-grandson, scanned the precious letter for me after I met him and his brothers Ranjit and Digvijay at Dhuru Lodge. Located a fifteen-minute walk away from Shivaji Park, it is a gracious two-storey bungalow, with a collonaded veranda on the ground floor, ornamental mouldings on the façade and vestiges of the old cottage at the back. A flight of wooden stairs leads to the living quarters. The living room should properly be called a diwankhana for its spaciousness, its dark, carved-wood furniture, its grandfather clock and its vintage cabinets. The warmth of the room is matched by the warmth of the Dhuru family's welcome. As we talk, it strikes me that the three brothers' names all stand for victory. Digvijay means conqueror of the universe; Ranjit, victor on the battlefield; and Ajit, one who is invincible. The Suryavanshi Kshatriyas were fighters by caste and proud of it. A tiny pamphlet written by Narayan Nathoba Patil records, rather ruefully,

'Once Muslim dynasties had conquered the country, Kshatriyas had no choice but to drop their swords and pick up the plough.' You cannot associate either sword or plough with the present generation of Dhurus. Living in their 250-year-old bungalow, which they have maintained in its pristine glory, they have moved with the times while carrying lightly the pride of being among the earliest settlers in Dadar.

Well before the Dhurus, Kavlis, Churis and Patils settled on the seaboard side of Dadar, a church had been built on the Gokhale Road side of Dadar by the Portuguese for its flock of Kolis converted to Christianity. This community was first known as Portuguese Christians, but were pushed to identify themselves more specifically when waves of Portuguese Christians or Goenkars began to arrive from Goa. So they assumed the name East Indians, colloquially Eastya, to assert their identity as natives of Bombay bearing allegiance to the East India Company and not Goenkars bearing allegiance to the Portuguese. The East Indians spoke a dialect of Marathi, mixed with Konkani and Portuguese. The Goenkars spoke Konkani.

The Nossa Senhora de Salvação, popularly known as Portuguese Church, was built in 1596. Salvasong, as that part of Dadar came to be called, was obviously a corruption of Salvação. Rebuilt four times between then

Swapnil Bhole

The Portuguese Church in its present avatar designed
by Charles Correa

and now, the church in its present avatar was designed by the internationally known architect Charles Correa. He completed the construction in 1977 and it instantly became a hotly debated subject among the parishioners and the cognoscenti. Its low-slung shell roofs in exposed reinforced cement concrete with no external embellishments and no spires was the last thing the regular church-goer expected God's house to be. Our neighbours, the Pereiras who had prayed at the old church, took a while to get used to the new one. Papa, Mama, sons and daughters-in-law had died. Only the two spinster daughters, Ursula and Ruby, remained. They went resignedly to the new church, dressed in their best frocks, carrying their head coverings and their Bibles.

When the whole family was alive and well, Mama Pereira would cook a special East Indian lunch on Sundays.

Its warm, spicy aromas would drift up into our kitchen. Ask daughter Ruby or daughter-in-law Sissy what spices Mama used and they would say bottle masala, which explained nothing. Decades later, Naresh Fernandes, a *Times of India* staffer, later author of *Taj Mahal Foxtrot* and founder-editor of the news website Scroll.in, brought me a small jar of the spice mix with the added bonus of his mother's recipe for lonvas, the East Indian meat-and-coconut-milk stew. As I stirred the bottle masala into the stew, I knew this was it. This was Sunday morning in Mama Pereira's kitchen.

4. The Birth of Shivaji Park

"'Sahib, I'm not a doctor like you, and I should not presume to tell you what you already know. In the past month more than fifty have died in my neighbourhood. Hale men and women, every one of them. Rich ghee-fed Marwari Jains like myself, not pathetic starvelings of the bazaar. Then, there are rumours."

"'Rumours?"

"'From the docks. The godowns are full of dead rats.'"

—*From* Room 000: Narratives of the Bombay Plague,
Kalpish Ratna

The outbreak of plague in Bombay in 1896 throws up a complex narrative of class, caste, community, tradition, ignorance and prejudice. The steps that the British government took to control the epidemic such as forcible examination, isolation and quarantine, caused intense anger among the citizens, many of whom fled to their villages to get away as much from the cure as the disease. This is not the place to enter into that labyrinth of cause and effect. What concerns us here is that Shivaji Park owes its birth, at least partly if not wholly, to the plague epidemic of 1896–97.

The problem created by the plague was not only socially complex, but medically too. There was a great resistance within the medical fraternity to accepting the new idea that baccilli were the cause of the disease. In every culture anywhere in the world, the plague had been seen as a divine retribution for man's sins. That superstition still clung to some medical men. Others resisted out of a sense of outrage that some whippersnappers were trying to sell them new-fangled theories. One such whippersnapper was Dr Sir Waldemar Mordecai Wolff Haffkine, whom the government had requested to help contain the epidemic. Haffkine started work in a poky corridor of the Grant Medical College in Byculla. In January 1897 he had a vaccine ready. He tested it on himself before trials were conducted on volunteers from Byculla jail. Those who were inoculated, survived the epidemic, while some members of the control group died. Haffkine arrived at the conclusion that the vaccine reduced risk by 50 per cent.

Disbelieving his findings, some officials insisted that the problem had to do entirely with the lack of sanitary conditions in the over-populated city. The belief led to the setting up of the Bombay City Improvement Trust (BCIT) on 9 December 1898. The Trust's first task was to build avenues across the length and breadth of the city to open up its landlocked central and eastern regions to healthful sea breezes. The roads would incidentally solve another problem that had been troubling the British rulers greatly. They would reduce the dense growth of toddy palms and coconut trees on the island. Not only did they block the free flow of sea air, but, worse still, their nurture created an unhealthy miasma on account of the local tradition of burying dried fish at their roots as manure. This noisome practice was held to be at least partly responsible for the rampant ill-health among the British, cutting their lives down to the proverbial two monsoons. The BCIT's second task was to create new areas for housing on Mahim island in order to decongest the city centre. This was to be achieved by reclaiming some land from the sea and acquiring some from the Koli, Bhandari, Suryavanshi and other landowners of the island.

The BCIT's first plans, known as Schemes 5 and 6, were designed to develop Dadar East, Matunga and Sion as residential precincts. An important feature of the schemes was building east-west roads that would release sea air to them. This entailed acquiring land from the landowners of the west. The landowners protested angrily. Why should they give up their land to benefit people living on the other side of the railway line? The land had been theirs 'from times immemorial' and they paid taxes on it. This gave them clout. Their anger culminated in a meeting held on the Dr Antonio da Silva grounds in 1915. A resolution was passed making their refusal to give up land for Schemes 5 and 6 clear, and demanding that a similar scheme be planned to develop Mahim Woods instead. In time the demand was granted and 'Shivaji Park Scheme-Mahim' for the development of one of the first planned precincts in the city was conceived.

Before the scheme took off, a prickly administrative issue had to be resolved. There had been growing friction between the BCIT, which had been constituted by an act of the British Parliament, and the Municipal Corporation whose councillors comprised the Indian elite of Bombay, including some landowners from Dadar West. By the end of the turf war, the BCIT was restricted to developing only the infrastructure—streets, drains, lighting—while the Municipal Corporation took charge of the development of the park and the sale of plots for housing. By 1936–37, all the plots around Shivaji Park were sold; and by 1940, plots on outlying roads which did not come under the Scheme but benefited from the infrastructure were also sold.

The layout of the Shivaji Park precinct comprises the park, covering an area of 112,937 square metres (27.907 acres), a stone and cement-concrete katta, or kerb, that encircles it fully and two roads that run around it in concentric horseshoes. What led to precisely this acreage of land being turned into a park is a matter for speculation. Two factors could have determined the specific location and area of the precinct. One, the existence of three thoroughfares that had already been constructed. Lady Jamshedji Road, bordering the eastern side of the precinct, was built in 1846. Mahim Bazaar Road on the west, once a mud track, had been widened into a proper road. It was renamed Cadell Road in 1916 after P.R. Cadell whose term as municipal commissioner had ended just then. The southern side was bounded by Ranade Road which stretched all the way from Dadar station to the beach, crossing three main roads—N.C. Kelkar Road, Gokhale Road and Cadell Road. The park along with its two horseshoe roads had to be contained within the boundaries set by these roads.

The actual area of the park was most likely determined by the grassy meadow that is said to have existed there before. Apparently, it was a commons that became squelchy and unusable in the monsoon months, but was used in the dry months as a camping site by itinerant traders, craftsmen and performers and as a meeting place for locals to celebrate festivals. Whether such a commons existed or not, the area of the park would have had to be contained within the two ring roads built for housing plots.

The park was thrown open to the public in 1925. It was first called Mahim Park. In 1927, the tercentenary year of Shivaji's birth, there was a popular demand for its renaming after him. The Congress corporator and Gandhian freedom fighter Avantikabai Gokhale gave voice to the people's demand and it was named Shivaji Park. This event is commemorated on a tall, wide column that stands with its back to the park and its face towards Cadell Road, renamed Veer Savarkar Marg. Currently it is in a soiled state, its base chipped and its sides plastered with the remains of handbills. A small peepal sapling has thrust itself out of a crack at the top. Our city fathers do not care very much for heritage.

Of the two ring roads, the innermost begins at Dadar beach as Keluskar Road South, cuts across Savarkar Marg, encircles the park, becomes Keluskar Road North, cuts across Savarkar Marg on the other side and ends at the beach. The second road begins at Savarkar Marg as Dr M.B. Raut Road South, encircles Keluskar Road, becomes Dr M.B. Raut Road North, cuts across Savarkar Marg and ends at the beach. Three short radial roads intersect the ring roads to the south, south-east and east to meet Ranade Road, the Shiv Sena Bhavan junction and Lady Jamshedji Road respectively.

Dr M.B. Raut Road was named after a Dadar resident who was not only a highly esteemed medical practitioner, but also associated with several social, cultural and sports organizations. As a municipal corporator, he paid particular attention to Dadar's development. The inner ring road is named after a Keluskar, not identified further by initials. Even *Bahurangi Bahudhangi Dadar*, which devotes a few lines to Dr M.B. Raut, says nothing about Keluskar. However,

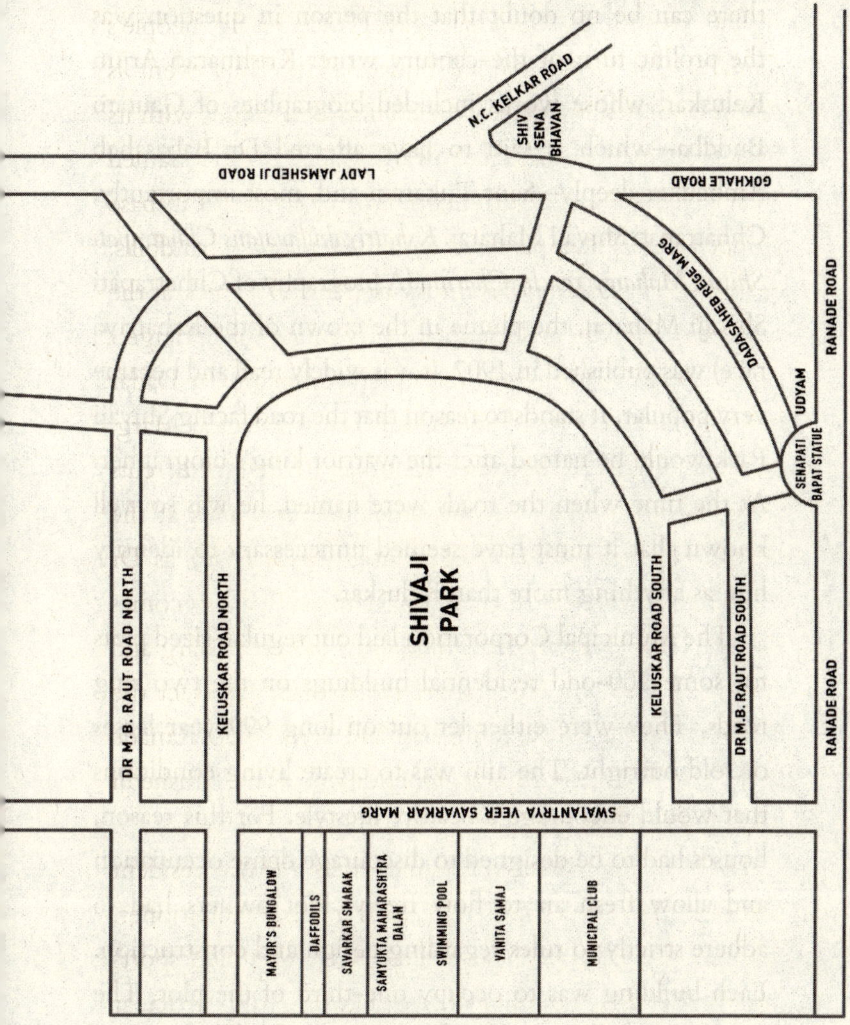

The author's impression of Shivaji Park

there can be no doubt that the person in question was the prolific turn-of-the-century writer Krishnarao Arjun Keluskar, whose works included biographies of Gautam Buddha—which is said to have affected Dr Babasaheb Ambedkar deeply—Sant Tukaram and, most importantly, Chhatrapati Shivaji Maharaj. *Kshatriyakulavatans Chhatrapati Shivaji Maharaj Yanche Charitra* (A biography of Chhatrapati Shivaji Maharaj, the plume in the crown of the Kshatriya race) was published in 1907. It was widely read and became very popular. It stands to reason that the road facing Shivaji Park would be named after the warrior king's biographer. At the time when the roads were named, he was so well known that it must have seemed unnecessary to identify him as anything more than Keluskar.

The Municipal Corporation laid out regular-sized plots for some 200-odd residential buildings on the two ring roads. They were either let out on long 999-year leases or sold outright. The aim was to create living conditions that would encourage a healthy lifestyle. For this reason, houses had to be designed to discourage dense occupation and allow fresh air to flow freely. Plot owners had to adhere strictly to rules regarding design and construction. Each building was to occupy one-third of the plot. The compound wall was to be 5 feet high at the back but a dwarf wall in front topped by a grill. The height of the building was to be no more than ground plus two or at most three floors. To ensure that the rules were followed, the Municipal

Corporation entered into lease or sale agreements only after the construction of the buildings had been completed according to rules.

Shivaji Park was designated a playground. A number of sports and cultural organizations were allowed to operate from small ground-floor structures along the inner periphery of the park. Of these the two that have had the widest impact nationally and internationally are the Samarth Vyayam Mandir at the south-west corner of the park and the Shivaji Park Gymkhana further along the south. Every evening sees children jumping, running, doing exercises and playing organized games at the Vyayamshala, while others practice on the mallakhamb. Uday Deshpande, the mallakhamb master-trainer, began his own training here at the age of three. He became so passionately committed to the sport, that he went beyond his own practice to become its worldwide ambassador. In the last twenty-five years he has taken the sport to many states outside Maharashtra and to fifty-two countries abroad. His efforts at popularizing mallakhamb culminated in the Samarth Vyayam Mandir hosting the first ever mallakhamb world championships from 16 to 17 February 2019 on its grounds. The championships were held under the auspices of the newly formed Vishwa Mallakhamb Federation (VMF) of which Deshpande is the secretary.

The Shivaji Park Gymkhana is known nationally as the cradle of Indian cricket. Some of the luminaries of test cricket, most notably Sandeep Patil, were coached here by Ankush

Saurab Rao

Young cricketers during a practice session

Vaidya, fondly called Anna. Established in 1909 as the New Maharashtra Cricket Club, the gymkhana had gone through several shifts from one plot to another in Dadar east till its fortunes changed with the development of Shivaji Park. R.K. Vaidya who was associated with the gymkhana and was also a municipal corporator connected with the scheme—a road that branches off Ranade Road is named after him—managed to get a small plot in Shivaji Park allotted to it. As the gymkhana's activities grew, it exchanged this plot for a larger one of some 4,200 square metres on the present site. The gymkhana was keen to have a pavilion but permission for a built structure inside the park was at first denied. Once again an ex-municipal corporator and former mayor, Dr M.C. Jawale, managed to obtain the required permission. The Shivaji Park Gymkhana building was inaugurated in 1932. In 1942, it managed to expand further. It now occupies 15,886 square metres of Shivaji Park land.

Saurab Rao

A gymnasium open for all

In keeping with the democratic nature of the park, there is an open gymnasium housed in a shed-like structure round the corner from the gymkhana on the east side of the park. Beginning with nothing more than parallel bars and rings, it now boasts of more varieties of apparatus that keep the working-class youth of the area fit.

Through the long summer vacation and the monsoon months, the muddy stretch of ground on the north side of the park is taken over by football clubs, one of the more well known being the Kenkre Football Academy.

On the west side of Shivaji Park going north from Samarth Vyayam Mandir are the other structures dedicated to sports and culture. After the Vyayamshala, comes the Maharashtra State Kabbadi Association. As a member of the all-India federation of the sport, it has been instrumental in making kabbadi popular worldwide. For many years now, a rhythmic gymnastics class is conducted on the terrace of the building, run by gymnast-coach Varsha Upadhye. In the early years, the class was held on the open ground in front of the Kabbadi Association. Watching from his wheelchair was Shankarrao Salvi, fondly known as Buwa Salvi and respectfully as Kabbadi Maharishi. One day he offered Upadhye the use of the Association's terrace, an offer she happily accepted. Ideally the training space for gymnastics should have a wooden floor and mirrors; but we are still a Third World country where sports facilities are concerned.

Next to the Kabbadi Association is the Mahim Juvenile Sports Club formed by a group of sports lovers in 1922. Initially housed near Dadar station, it moved later to Shivaji Park. The club participates in cricket and table tennis tournaments and holds coaching classes for young cricketers. It also hires out its premises for trendy fitness dance classes. A few years ago it used to be aerobics. Presently it is zumba.

Sharing its northside wall is the Shivaji Park Nagarik Sangh, which was also formed by a group of like-minded citizens in 1947. This was clearly a time when ordinary citizens could come together and form organizations without financial help from the government. Most clubs in Shivaji Park live off life memberships, corporate patronage and rentals. The Shivaji Park Nagarik Sangh organizes lectures on civic subjects and hosts gatherings on festival days. For the last few years Amarendra Nandu Dhaneshwar, a Gwalior gharana vocalist, born and brought up on Dr M.B. Raut Road but now a resident of Mahim, has been curating classical music concerts in the Sangh's hall. On mornings when it is not too cold or wet, a bunch of RSS old-timers gathers in the paved space beside the Sangh. They recite their morning prayer and sometimes do some physical exercises.

Standing quietly beside Nagarik Sangh is an interesting piece of antiquity: a piyaav or drinking fountain. This is one of thirty or so piyaavs that have been documented so far in

Saurab Rao

The basalt stone piyaav

Mumbai city. About 4 feet in height, this simple basalt stone piyaav with an ordinary spout and spill-over basin is inlaid with a marble plaque that names Mr Ramji Setiba as the donor but says nothing about the date of its construction. Given that it faces neither the park nor the road, I would like to believe it was made for the people who camped here when the place was still a commons.

Between the Nagarik Sangh and the Udyan Ganapati temple lies the beautifully manicured garden memorial to Balasaheb Thackeray who died on 17 November 2012 and was cremated at the spot. Permission was granted for his cremation in Shivaji Park after several rules standing in the way were pushed through loopholes. The main reason given by the police for bending rules was that the Bhagoji Keer Crematorium near Dadar beach would be too small to hold the thousands of mourners who were expected to attend the funeral and could lead to a breakdown of law and order. VIP security would also be difficult to organize under the circumstances. Once permission was granted for cremation in Shivaji Park, the inevitable demand followed—a memorial at the spot. Since a public playground is no place for memorials to politicians, the garden was made as a stop-gap compromise, till space could be found for a permanent memorial.

A 20-foot equestrian statue of Shivaji towers over the memorial garden. The warrior has not been depicted with drawn sword as is customary. Instead, his right arm

Swapnil Bhole

The statue of Shivaji towering over Balasaheb Thacakery's memorial garden

is raised as though to give direction to his people. The behind-the-scenes story of the making of the statue appears in *Drishyakala*, an encyclopaedia of artists of Maharashtra edited by Suhas Bahulkar and Deepak Ghare. After Narayan Ganesh Pansare, the sculptor, had completed a plaster of Paris replica of the statue, the statue committee decided it would have to be bigger in order not to look insignificant in the enormous expanse of the park. Pansare was reluctant to increase its height. The encyclopeadia does not say why. But it could be because funds collected from the public for the statue would not have covered the increased height. The date for the unveiling had already been fixed. Under tremendous pressure, Pansare saw no other way out but to sink his life's savings into the work. The statue was unveiled on schedule on 6 November 1966. 'But,' says the encyclopedia, 'it left Pansare a financially and emotionally broken man.' He died of a massive heart attack on 24 May 1968.

We are now on a stretch that tells us how big Shivaji Park is on religion. The Udyan Ganapati beyond the Shivaji statue comes with a legend attached. A beautiful idol of Ganapati is said to have miraculously appeared one day under an old banyan tree. There is certainly a banyan tree nearby which could be the one. The idol began to be worshipped. As its fame grew, a small shrine was built to house it. Soon it acquired a name, Udyan Ganapati, Ganapati of the Park. The shrine became famous when word went around that the deity granted people's wishes. This brought in more devotees and more donations. A few years ago marble slabs and marble carvers from Rajasthan appeared. The small temple gave way to a larger, more splendid one. It stands with its back to Savarkar Marg, which means walkers do not see the idol as they pass by. But they stop by all the same to fold their hands and mutter a prayer.

The Kali temple next door faces the road, the idol of the rather benign-looking goddess glints under the temple light. A small crowd of people attends morning aartis sung rather tunelessly, I think, to the accompaniment of drum and conch. The temple belonged to the Bengal Club next door, before a trust was formed to manage its affairs. The

Bengal Club was established in 1922. It describes itself on its website as 'the homing ground for Bengalis across Mumbai'. Every year come Durga Puja, it takes over a large area of Shivaji Park adjoining the club house for its celebrations, attended by huge crowds who shop, eat, watch cultural programmes and gaze with awe upon the resplendent Durga idol.

Beyond the Kali temple, in the north-west corner of the park, directly outside the Maharashtra State Bharat Scouts & Guides is the Holy Cross Chapel. It is a small, unpretentious structure comprising a statue of Jesus on the cross sheltered by a hood. The chapel has evolved from a tiny INRI cross which was erected they say for the benefit of Catholic ayahs

Saurab Rao

The C. Ramchandra Memorial, the Holy Cross and the Scouts Pavilion, all huddled together in the north-west corner of Shivaji Park

who worked for film actors and producers living on that side of the park. Today people of all faiths and communities stop to cross themselves before the statue.

The Scouts Pavilion, as it is locally known, is involved with basic training and refresher courses for Scout leaders. This and its association with the international Scouts and Guides movement are its core but hidden activities. Its visible activity is the hiring out of its spacious hall for weddings and exhibitions.

Till a few years ago a Ram Leela troupe used to perform regularly on a makeshift stage in the north-east corner of the park. It does not perform there any longer. An annual Jagannath Yatra has been allowed to use the space instead, much to the chagrin of citizens who are ever vigilant against the park being used as anything other than a playground. The yatra is spectacular, noisy, and causes huge traffic jams when it takes out its annual procession around the Dadar-Prabhadevi area.

Going south from here on the east side of the park, beyond the open gymnasium, are two gardens, one for senior citizens and the other for children. That completes the inner periphery of Shivaji Park.

Let us step out of the park now, cross Savarkar Marg and look at the Mayor's Bungalow, or what used to be the Mayor's bungalow. Unlike the planned houses around Shivaji Park which flaunt Art Deco features, this bungalow defies architectural description. Or so I thought,

The Mayor's Bungalow

till architect, teacher, poet and translator, Mustansir Dalvi found words for it. 'It is an eclectic mix,' he said to me in an email, 'although the predominant style is the neo-Baroque, with other neo-classical features. This is seen in the idiosyncratic shapes of the arches as well as the copious floral ornamentation between them. Even the keystones to the arches are highlighted. The columns have Corinthian [leafy] capitals. The use of stone brackets is also an indicator. There are no pointed arches, spires, towers or buttresses to indicate a neo-Gothic styling. The closest to the neo-Gothic is the timber staircase in the interior.' Dalvi ended the description with a terse summing up, easy for the layperson to understand: 'It is a bit of a khichdi.'

Built in 1928, the ground-plus-one structure was once

home to a princess of the royal house of Bikaner. At some point, the British took it over for storing official documents. The Bombay Municipal Corporation bought it in 1962 to serve as the mayor's official residence. Occupying an area of 4,500 square feet, with two halls, two bedrooms, a VIP room, a study and a kitchen, set on 2.75 acres of land, it is an imposing enough edifice for Mumbai's first citizen to live in.

After Balasaheb Thackeray, the Hindu Hriday Samrat and erstwhile supremo of the Shiv Sena, died, party seniors led by his son Uddhav, began looking for a suitable structure to convert into an appropriately grand memorial for him. The Mayor's Bungalow struck them as just the right choice. Negotiations lasted for six years till the required permission was officially granted by the state. But there was a hitch. The bungalow is a heritage structure which cannot be touched. A solution has been found for that. It has been decided that the larger part of the memorial will be built underground with the bungalow itself serving as extra space.

On Monday 21 January 2019, Mumbai's first citizen and seventy-sixth mayor Vishwanath Mahadeshwar shifted to a temporary accommodation in the Veermata Jijabai Bhosle Udyan and Zoo complex at Byculla. There a bungalow occupied by a top government official was vacated for his use. Special sound barriers have been erected around it to ensure that he is not disturbed by animal calls from the zoo. Meanwhile the BMC (Brihanmumbai Municipal Corporation) is said to be constructing a new official bungalow for the mayor at Shivaji Park or in its vicinity.

Next door to the Thackeray memorial-in-the-making is a small plot of land lush with vegetation and trees. Standing in the dappled light is a small building which houses Daffodils, a playschool and kindergarten that the Keraleeya Mahila Samaj has been running for fifty-five years. Some elderly residents of Shivaji Park and their sons and daughters learned their ABC here. Now their grandchildren are doing the same. The plot, leased to the Mahila Samaj by the BMC, is currently being sought as additional space for the Thackeray memorial. The BMC has offered them alternative plots elsewhere but the Samaj has turned them down. The case is in the courts.

Beside Daffodils stands the imposing Swatantrya Veer Savarkar Rashtriya Smarak. The idea for such a memorial to V.D. Savarkar was mooted after he passed away on 26 February 1966 at his home on Dr M.B. Raut Road. The BMC handed over this 6,650 square metres plot to the Rashtriya Smarak Trust at a nominal lease rent. The building came up in stages as and when funds became available. It was inaugurated on 28 May 1989 by the then president of India, Shankar Dayal Sharma, in the presence of the governor of Maharashtra, Brahmananda Reddy and the chief minister Sharad Pawar. Until recently one could see Savarkar's statue, installed on the first-floor terrace

Saurab Rao

Vinayak Damodar Savarkar's statue against the painting of Bharat Mata

against a painting of Bharat Mata, from across the road. It is now blocked from view by seating arrangements for an interactive show on Savarkar's life and work.

Next to the Savarkar Smarak is the all-white Samyukta Maharashtra Smruti Dalan. This basement, ground and first-floor structure houses an exhibition on the history of the United Maharashtra agitation that led to the formation of the linguistic state of Maharashtra on 1 May 1960. The structure includes the entrance to the Mahatma Gandhi Olympic Swimming Pool at the back. The pool was inaugurated on 27 April 1952. In its first thirty years, it produced several champion swimmers. Later, with the sea eating into its walls, it went into long bouts of repairs that destroyed its national status. It reopened in 2006 as a pool that had lost its Olympian shine.

Next to the swimming pool is a wooded property belonging to an Irani family, the Kermanis. Beside it is Vanita Samaj, a meeting place for Shivaji Park's homemakers. Lakshmibai Modak, wife of the then city engineer N.V. Modak, founded the club in 1937. An unassuming structure at first, it was soon replaced by a graceful bungalow with a pitched roof and wrap-around veranda. A few years later, it acquired an indoor badminton court where an annual national tournament was held, attracting the top shuttling talent of the country. The last addition to the property was a 1000-seater auditorium which, along with the lawn in front of it, has become the most desired venue for middle-class weddings. The old bungalow was demolished a few years ago to be replaced by a less graceful but more functional one-storeyed building.

Beyond the Samaj is the Municipal Employees' Sports Club which looks decrepit now but once buzzed with activity on its badminton and tennis courts. Turn the corner from here into the beachside stretch of Keluskar Road South and you are next to a beautiful park known to the locals as Narali Baag, because of the numerous coconut trees that sway amongst its well laid-out paths. Like many gardens in Mumbai, Narali Baag too has a bandstand where no band plays.

Across the road from the park is a narrow lane leading to the crematorium. This is where leaders like Sane Guruji and Dr Ambedkar were cremated. The crematorium was built with a generous donation from an affluent contractor named Bhagoji Keer who came to Bombay as a callow youth from Ratnagiri, with little education and no experience of life beyond his home town. He found work with the construction firm Shapurji Pallonji, learned the ropes on the job, worked hard and soon established himself independently as a contractor. A bust of Bhagoji Keer has been installed on the corner of the crematorium lane in gratitude for his philanthropy.

A crematorium makes a fitting if somewhat macabre end to this part of the Shivaji Park story. But I intend continuing for a bit longer. What strikes you most forcibly about Shivaji Park, besides its shady roads and Art Deco buildings, is the openness of the space. By that I do not mean the obvious, as in a space that is not enclosed. I mean open as in democratic. Shivaji Park is open to all people at all times of the day and night. It is a place to relax in and fill your lungs with fresh air, to hold hands or argue, walk, jog, do asanas or stretch out for a siesta. It is open for post-prandial strolls under the stars or for indulgences like ice golas sold off carts.

The Shivaji Park katta is a beloved seating and sleeping arrangement. No recollection of the park is complete without memories of katta days flooding in. The katta is just a low kerb around the park. But what possibilities it affords for human interaction! In a blogpost reproduced in *Firstpost*, Mustansir Dalvi compares the snooty Oval maidan at Churchgate with Shivaji Park. The Oval, he says, 'is fenced off with railings that put you in mind of a penitentiary no matter which side you are on…What could have been, in the absence of the railings, a positive social space, a "living room for the city", for all those with purpose and for flaneurs in general, is now fossilized for the rather vapid pleasure of viewing from the balconies of Deco residences.' The Shivaji Park katta on the other hand affords 'unfiltered access from all sides, allowing an extended neighbourhood to occupy it and call it their own'.

Those who have lived in this neighbourhood but moved away still feel this sense of ownership. To come back to Shivaji Park and shoot the breeze on the katta is like returning home. Today the BMC, in its unaesthetic wisdom, has covered this home with glossy plastic chips in ugly orange, yellow and red instead of the dull green paint we were used to and which fitted better with the surroundings. The chips are already falling out. One hopes they will all be gone one day.

5. Shivaji Park's First Citizen

'A bungalow at Shivaji Park built in the 1930's.'

—Caption for a photograph of Udyam,
Bombay: The Cities Within, *Sharda Dwivedi,*
Rahul Mehrotra

'However good and accurate an engineer may be, he will not succeed unless he knows thoroughly well how to present his facts. His first and foremost consideration should be the good of the locality and he should use his influence with the council to secure his end.'

—From a speech by N.V. Modak delivered at the 30th Indian Science Congress, Calcutta, 1943

Reading the chapter entitled 'Exploding City Imploding Centre' in Sharda Dwivedi and Rahul Mehrotra's gorgeously illustrated book *Bombay: The Cities Within*, I come upon a picture on page 265 captioned as above. A bungalow? Just that and no more? But that is N.V. Modak's bungalow Udyam. It is a landmark in Shivaji Park. No, in the whole of Dadar. In the old days, perhaps even now, if you said you lived near Modak engineer's bungalow, people knew where that was.

Udyam once housed city engineer N.V. Modak's extended family. No Modak lives in the bungalow now, only two tenant families in the left wing. The right wing is occupied by Dr Avinash Phadke's well-known and well-regarded pathology laboratory. Dr Phadke is a relation of the Modaks. There used to be a municipal school on the ground floor of Udyam which shut down many years ago. The lease granted to the Brihanmumbai Municipal Corporation has expired, but it had refused to surrender the space till recently. For many years it was the constituency's voting centre. That once-in-five-years exercise is also history. So, in a city starved for space, the doors of the school remain locked.

I visit Dr Prasad Modak, son of N.V. Modak's youngest brother Madhav, also a public health engineer. The widely travelled Dr Modak is the executive president of his own organization, Environmental Management Centre, and author of several publications. Dr Modak and his ceramist wife Kiran live on the third floor of a spacious double apartment in one of Shivaji Park's newer buildings, a seven-storey structure on Dr M.B. Raut Road. Other new buildings on this road and on Keluskar Road stand twenty or more storeys high.

Speaking about his uncle's town planning vision, Dr Modak leads me into the veranda to see how the housing plots facing each other on Raut Road are staggered. This simple ploy has ensured free flow of air from the park to homes on Dr Modak's side of the road. It is not only Shivaji Park but Dadar as a whole that owes much to N.V. Modak's engineering enterprise. He conceived and built Dadar's sewage and sewerage plant, which indirectly led to Calcutta's wetlands being preserved. Gandhian ecologist Sopan Joshi narrates how it happened in his obituary for Dhrubajyoti Ghosh in *The Indian Express* dated 20 February 2018:

'Sometime in the early 1980s, West Bengal's finance minister wanted to find out how to gainfully use Kolkata's sewage. Dhrubajyoti Ghosh, an engineer in the state's planning board, was assigned the task. He was to travel across the country and prepare a report within a year. He got his ticket to visit India's first sewage treatment plant at Dadar, Mumbai. Then came a moment of introspection. "It occurred to me that they might ask me how Kolkata handles its sewage," Ghosh later recounted. "I didn't know." He searched high and low and found nothing. It seemed nobody knew what the city did with its sewage. So Ghosh did what officers aren't encouraged to do in government policy: He went for a walk. He ambled along the 28-km channel that carried the city's sewage eastwards, along the slope, to where the salt marshes once stood. Here, he saw shallow ponds that turned the city's sewage into algae. Then, the algae-rich water was let into nurseries, to be eaten by fish, that was then sold in the city. A marvel of recycling, of turning waste into food. Ghosh ended up dedicating most of his working life to the wetlands... That the East Kolkata Wetlands (EKW) exist today, spread over thousands of acres, owes to Ghosh's untiring efforts.'

Nanasaheb, as N.V. Modak was known, had to fight hard to prove that the Dadar sewage plant was worth the huge cost the municipal corporation was bearing for it. Citizens had to be convinced that their money was not being wasted on human waste. Dr Modak tells me a story in this regard. 'The clamour of the citizens culminated in a demand that a public meeting be held in Shivaji Park to allow citizens to ask my uncle questions regarding the plant. The meeting was well attended. Uncle was asked many technical questions which he answered. But one gentleman asked him how they could be sure the sewage treatment did indeed clean it of all impurities. The treated water was actually meant chiefly for use in textile mills and did not have to be drinkable. However, my uncle decided to create a moment of drama. He said, "The treated water is clean enough even to drink." He called for a glass of the water and took a couple of sips from it. The sceptical gentleman was convinced.'

By the 1990s, the plant had served its purpose. It was shut down in 1999 but its stink remained. In 2007, the Sewage Operations Department (SOD) of the BMC decided to convert the 10-acre plot into a garden. Inaugurated in 2014 and named after the late Pramod Mahajan of the Bharatiya Janata Party, the SOD has added two lakh trees to the hundred and more that already existed. Flowerbeds, walking paths, a children's play area and benches make this green lung a great place to relax in. The treated water from the pumping system that still exists is used to water the garden. The excess is supplied to neighbouring gardens.

What the entire city, not just Dadar, have to thank N.V. Modak for is the Vaitarna Dam, named Modak Sagar after him. It was built to augment the city's water supply when the supply from Vihar, Tulsi and Tansa lakes taken together still fell short of the city's constantly growing requirements. *The Economic Weekly* dated 26 October 1954 carried a report which said, 'In February 1947, Shri N V Mockik [sic], the Special Engineer of the Bombay Municipal Corporation, submitted to the Corporation the outline of a scheme for creating a reservoir on the Vaitarna river by constructing a dam along with a diversion tunnel of the required capacity for linking this reservoir with the Tansa lake. The Corporation sanctioned the survey work and preparation of a detailed scheme in July 1948. The scheme, as drawn up with estimates, received the sanction of the Corporation soon.'

The Vaitarna dam was the first in the country to be constructed using pre-cooled concrete. Nanasaheb studied the advanced technology and decided to set up an ice-plant on the site to facilitate the cooling process. The Project Completion Report that Nanasaheb submitted to the Municipal Corporation in 1957 makes fascinating reading. It gives us an idea of the technological challenges and labour that went into ensuring that water flowed out of our taps when we opened them.

There is a story behind the designation Special Engineer by which Modak is referred to in *The Economic Weekly* report. Nanasaheb was working with the Great Indian Peninsula Railway Company, a private enterprise, when he was appointed deputy chief engineer in the Bombay Municipal Corporation. This was around 1931. He was promoted to the post of city engineer in 1932. He served in this capacity till 1947, when he was appointed municipal commissioner. He resigned from the city engineer's post in order to take over as commissioner. However, Corporation rules stipulated that only Indian civil servants could hold this office. So Nanasaheb had to relinquish it within four months of his appointment and found himself in limbo. But not for long. He was soon designated Special Engineer with a salary of Rs 3000, equal to the commissioner's. He served the BMC in this capacity till he retired in 1955.

It is never easy for visionary engineers who work for governments and municipalities to put their ideas into practice. But Modak was always clear about his priorities. We see this in his address at the 30th Indian Science Congress held in Calcutta in 1943: 'Coming now to the Municipal Engineer, his position today is not happy. He has not infrequently to regret that a solution or a step recommended by him as proper and fitting, is delayed or abandoned for some reason or the other. He should not, however, get discouraged, but should try to steadily put forth his point of view on every possible occasion; and this he can only do if he were able to write an intelligent report explaining in concise and logical order the details of the case entrusted to him. However good and accurate an engineer may be, he will not succeed unless he knows thoroughly well how to present his facts. His first and foremost consideration should be the good of the locality and he should use his influence with the council to secure his end. As a public official, he is in the public eye, and naturally he is subject to criticism, just and unjust. Here he should develop the quality of not being too sensitive and should take no heed of the unjust criticism so long he is carrying out his duties loyally, faithfully and to the best of his ability as per the policy enunciated by the local authority under which he is serving and so long as his character and integrity are of a high order.'

Character and integrity are no longer words we hear pronounced by those who serve the city.

6. They Came to Stay

'Much of my adult life was spent in the very heart of Girgaon "where Kandewadi kicks off lightly from Thakurdwar". The chawls in this culturally homogeneous neighbourhood were the stronghold of the Marathi lower-middle class. Some of the residents were to fan out later into the suburbs, to live in what were known disapprovingly as "blocks". The disapproval stemmed from the assertion of individualism that blocks were perceived to be making against the community life of chawls. In chawls, doors remained wide open till bedtime. If some residents misguidedly assumed the ways of the sahib and kept their doors closed in the day, they soon heard contemptuous remarks like "Tell them to go live in a block".'*

'Uncle left our chawl under the pretext of his job with the railways. If we, in childlike innocence, said to Father, "Dada,

*The opening line of an untitled poem by Marathi's first modernist poet, B.S. Mardhekar, which goes, 'Where Kandewadi kicks off lightly from Thakurdwar / There runs the tram / Bent at the waist / Rattling and licking the overhead flex'.

let's leave this place for something more spacious. Maybe in Dadar. They say there are nice places there. And inexpensive too," the attempt proved futile. The very manner in which Dada pronounced the word Dadar, implied his utter contempt for a place that was so remote, it might as well lie beyond Thane creek. "I am not going to budge from here," he would say stolidly, adding for good measure, "Go where you like when you grow up and get too smart for your boots and start making more money than is good for you. Go to your Dadar...or better still...go rot in Andheri.'

—'The Last Tram' from 'Nivdak Kharde',
M.V. Rajadhyaksha

'But what is heartening is that despite the widespread urbanisation, pockets of the city still retain their old-world charm and culture. The chawl culture—unique to Mumbai—practices the most important religion, the religion of loving and caring for your neighbours. Every festival and occasion, good or bad, is celebrated together. And the common corridor toilets—much hated by young people these days—have been the venue of many a love story. These romances often progressed to what we called tumbrel marriages, which the entire chawl celebrated with great gusto.'*

—Shiv Sena leader Pramod Navalkar's guest column,
India Today, *14 August 2006*

*Chawls have common toilets on each floor. The word 'tumbrel' is a corruption of the English word 'tumbler'. Chawl dwellers carried large mugs to the toilet to wash up.

THE CONVIVIALITY OF CHAWLS WAS, TILL RECENTLY, THE source of instant nostalgia among the middle classes. The chawl was a typology that suited them to a T. They had arrived in Bombay during the late 19th and early 20th centuries from villages where the community spirit was vigorously alive and where everybody was an authorized busybody. Community life became even more fruitful in chawls when matrons stood in toilet queues exchanging gossip and young girls and boys whispered sweet nothings. Gossip produced delicious rumours. P.L. Deshpande, Maharashtra's beloved humorist, has a story in which a chawl resident hears a hurtful rumour about a neighbour suspecting him of having pinched his 'tumbrel'.

Moving from a chawl where such jolly things were happening to a block where you were not supposed to know what was cooking in your neighbour's kitchen, was not just a change of living space. It was a traumatic shift from a native culture to an alien one. But 'blocks' were mushrooming all over Dadar, Mahim, Matunga and Sion, and people were slowly beginning to see the benefits of moving. Some made the move happily; others reluctantly, forced by circumstances, and some resisted. 'To Let' signs were everywhere in the initial years of Shivaji Park's development. So what were the reasons that prompted people to make the move? Here is a very small sample of stories that Shivaji Park residents tell.

Consumer activist Ashok Ravat's father Kashinath once

lived in Girgaum. Unlike many others, he saw sense in the Municipal Corporation's scheme for decongesting the 'native' town and creating a new neighbourhood of well-planned housing in what was once Lower Mahim and now Dadar. With the memory of the plague still hanging like a dark cloud over the city, it was foolish not to move to a more open space where you could live a healthy life. Empty plots were available to be bought or leased. Kashinath Ravat moved from Girgaum to a plot on Keluskar Road North and built a single-storey cottage for the family in 1936. He called it Dadaji Nishant after his father. It is a cosy-looking bungalow with a curved façade and plenty of garden space at the back. There is also the Arabian Sea, a five-minute

Saurab Rao

Dadaji Nishant, one of the oldest bungalows in the Shivaji Park precinct walk away on the other side of Savarkar Marg. And the great big park spread out in front.

Ashok Ravat was one of nine siblings. Inevitably, at some point, Dadaji Nishant began to burst at the seams. A division of Kashinath Ravat's property followed. The bungalow went to one of Ravat's siblings and he moved to Buildarch Olive, a thirteen-storey tower on Dadasaheb Rege Marg, bang opposite N.V.Modak's Udyam. From the window of his eighth-floor flat, I cast my eyes over the wide stretch of the neighbourhood that is on view, over the tops of buildings in Patil Wadi and Paralkar Marg, down the left flank of Ranade Road all the way to the beach.

The seventy-seven-year-old Ravat, tall and soft-spoken, has fought consistently for the rights of Shivaji Park's citizens. For a few years after his father passed away, he had taken over his real estate business. 'In those days,' says Ravat, 'business transactions were straightforward and clean.' However, after the Emergency he saw that you could no longer do business without greasing palms. So he gave up the real estate business to become a full-time activist. He has headed a number of citizens' movements like the Mumbai Grahak Panchayat, the All-India Bank Depositors' Association, the Citizens' Forum of G/North Ward, the Shivaji Park Advanced Locality Movement and the Walkers Ecological Movement (WECOM). In 1979, when he was fighting against a certain illegal construction in Shivaji Park, he found himself in the crosshairs of a politician who was involved in the project. He learned from a reliable source that the politician had hired contract killers to eliminate him. In a story headlined 'The Guardian Angel of Shivaji Park', published in *The Free Press Journal* dated 2 March 2013, Ravat is quoted as saying, 'In those days, a black car used to shadow me. But I refused to budge from my stand.' His stand paid off and the project had to be dropped.

In 2009, Ravat helped WECOM file a PIL in the Bombay High Court against the noise pollution caused by loudspeakers used during political rallies and other events in Shivaji Park. The PIL resulted in the park being declared a noise-free zone. Despite this, WECOM have had to return to the High Court repeatedly with complaints against infringements of the judgement. The Jagannath Yatra, for instance, had used loudspeakers without applying for permission. The police had taken action against the organizers, but only under the mild Maharashtra Police Act, 1951, without combining it with the Environment (Protection) Act, 1986 and the Noise Pollution Rules, 2000. The High Court pulled up the police for having failed to do their duty.

Champak, a striking two-storey building, stands across the park from Dadaji Nishant. Like many other houses in the precinct, Champak too was built in 1937. But its occupants, unlike many others, did not move from a congested area in south Bombay, but from outside the city. Vishwanath Chaubal, who rented a flat on the first floor of the building, had been a district judge. During his professional life he had been posted to courts all over Bombay Presidency. His last posting had been in Solapur. When he needed to decide where to settle down after he retired, he chose Bombay. It was after all, the city of gold and he had heard that a most inviting new neighbourhood called Shivaji Park was being developed there. The thought that his only son Vasant, then nineteen, might soon be looking for a job and there could be no better place than Bombay for that, could have played a part in his choice. There were many empty buildings in Shivaji Park waiting to be bought and flats waiting to be rented. Anuradha Shah, Vasant Chaubal's daughter, says Prabhat building down the road was on sale and her grandfather had momentarily toyed with the idea of buying it. But finally he chose Champak which was owned by a relative who had offered him the first-floor flat. Vasant and his wife Sheela lived there all their lives with their elder daughter Swaroop and younger daughter Anuradha. Both daughters have since moved away and so have the owners on the second floor. Almost empty as it now is, it has held its ground against redevelopment. It has been graded 'Good' in the report on Shivaji Park presented to the Mumbai Metropolitan Region–Heritage Conservation Society by Adarkar Associates in April 2014. 'Good' and the other grades 'Basic' and 'Fair' denote to what degree a building approximates to the stipulated ratios of built form to plot size and road width, and to the predominant architectural language of the precinct, Art Deco. Dadaji Nishant is also marked 'Good'.

❧

How the Dhaneshwars came to occupy Desai Cottage on Dr M.B. Raut Road, a ground-plus-three building—not at all like a cottage as its name suggests—is a third kind of story. Dwarkanath Dhaneshwar was born in Ahmednagar and went to college in Pune. He had arrived in Bombay in 1944 in search of work. He and his wife Jayashree, a Pune girl, lived in a small room in a large chawl in Girgaum's Paan Gully. Amarendra Nandu Dhaneshwar, Gwalior Gharana vocalist and music critic who grew up in Desai Cottage, says, 'In 1954, my father who was PA to Yeshwantrao Chavan heard on the government grapevine that blocks were being requisitioned in Shivaji Park for government servants. So he took the opportunity to move to this place.'

The house was called Sushi Kunj then. It was a ground-plus-two building owned by one Mr Bhatkal, a keen racegoer. Initially when they moved, the Dhaneshwars were given only one back room and a kitchen on the ground floor.

'Why did your father want to move from one small room to another?'

Dhaneshwar laughs. 'I suspect it was because my mother,

who had lived in a proper house in Pune, couldn't endure the common toilet in the chawl.' The one-room-kitchen accommodation in Sushi Kunj had an independent toilet. Soon the tenants in the front rooms moved out and the Dhaneshwars were given the entire ground-floor flat.

'And when did Sushi Kunj become Desai Cottage?'

'In 1960 after Ramakant Desai became a test cricketer.'

'Excuse me. What's the connection?'

'Cricketers didn't make as much money then as they do now. But Ramakant must have made some, because his father Bhikaji Desai bought Sushi Kunj. The Desais were a large family and needed more space than they had in their chawl near Plaza cinema. In those days it was the practice for landlords to occupy the topmost floor. But here that floor was already occupied. So Bhikaji Desai built a third floor for himself.'

The Shivaji Park neighbourhood continued to develop after the houses on the ring roads were built and occupied. My house Lalit Estate was built in 1940 on what was then known as Bhandarwada Road after the Bhandaris who populated the area. Across the road from us was Rath Wadi. The owner's cottage was tucked away deep among the coconut trees. Nearer to the edge of the wadi was a row of huts occupied by Bhandari toddy-tappers. Rath Wadi retained its character through my school years, even after the cyclone of 1948 had felled many of its coconut trees. It began changing only after the '60s. Gradually, the owner's cottage, the Bhandaris' huts and the coconut trees made way for the apartment buildings which stand there today.

When Rath Wadi was still a wadi, it offered us children exciting entertainment every Shimga, the five-day Holi festival celebrated in Konkan where the Bhandaris originated. Troupes of Naman Khele performers, a folk performance from the Konkan, would come to the wadi then. The performer who most excited us was Shankhasur. Dressed in a long black cloak girdled by heavy bells, he wore a conical hat covered by a black, face-covering veil with two scary holes for eyes. He carried a rope whip which he would swing at us as we ran behind him screaming. The rest of the troupe, dressed in long white frock coats with colourful cummerbunds, red stoles draped round their shoulders and bells on their ankles, swayed in a line singing their ritual song to the accompaniment of cymbals and drum. Vijay Tendulkar got his idea for the line of swaying, singing brahmins in *Ghashiram Kotwal* from a Naman Khele performance he saw in a Vile Parle wadi. Shivaji Park is still visited by other folk performers from the residents' village roots. The Nandi Bailwalla comes regularly with his richly caparisoned bull and so does the Vasudev.

I have no village roots. My father came to Lalit Estate, Shivaji Park via Belgaum where he was born, Dharwad where he went to college and Patna where he found his first foothold in journalism. He came to Bombay in 1941 when he was appointed 'Journalist' in the Bombay government's Directorate of Information. When he rented the first floor 'block' in Lalit Estate, the building was one year old and I was two. The design of the flat proves how abundant space was in Shivaji Park eighty years ago. A builder who came to assess its redevelopment possibilities, almost wept over the 'wasted' space. 'You could get a three-bedroom flat out of this,' he kept saying as he walked about with sad eyes. True. Our single bedroom with odd corners and curves must be at least 300 square feet in area and the veranda another 200. Although its exaggerated curves and flat chhajas mark Lalit Estate as Art Deco-inspired, it is located on the outskirts of the planned precinct, where the precinct's rules did not apply. The building covers the entire plot with no more than an 18-inch strip left free at the back. The builder, who wept over wasted space in Lalit Estate, went away weeping even more over the absence of surrounding space that would allow him an extra bit of Floor Space Index to make redevelopment profitable. The building is non-redevelopable. This is bad news for the cousins who own the property. One is the original owner and famous actor Shanta Apte's daughter. The other is the daughter of the brother who managed her affairs. Through all the changes of ownership that followed Shanta Apte's death in 1964, we, the tenants of Lalit Estate, have been the effective owners. Together, we have paid the water bills, installed new amenities, repaired the building when required, and had it painted. Our structural engineer has informed us that Lalit Estate is good for another few decades if it is maintained in this way. Many of the buildings in Shivaji Park that have been demolished were also built to last. But 'development' does not take congnisance of inconvenient facts.

The old Bhandarwada Road ended at Lalit Estate. Beyond it lay a kutcha road that curved around Rath Wadi to join Cadell Road. Bhandarwada Road was metalled in the late '60s and named Shankarrao Harishchandra Paralkar Marg. Paralkar was a well-known architect and a lecturer at the Sir J.J. School of Architecture. As president of the Indian Institute of Architects, he was involved with the construction of Shivaji Park's premier theatre, Shivaji Mandir. To the left of Bhandarwada Road, where it curved, lay Churi Wadi and Fernandes Wadi on either side of a dirt track. A large part of Churi Wadi was acquired by the Institute of Hotel Management, Catering Technology and Applied Nutrition in the 1970s. In the same decade, plots were sold for residential buildings in Fernandes Wadi.

Govindrao Bhide came to stay in one of the Fernandes Wadi buildings in 1973. 'When we moved in, there was no approach road to our buildings from the Bhandarwada Road end,' Bhide told me during our morning walk. 'We had to take a circuitous route from the other end to get there.'

Years later, the dirt path of the old wadi became Bhikoba Pathare Marg, named after a local social worker. The Bhides came from an extended family that had occupied a sprawling house near the well-known Shastri Hall in Nana Chowk, Tardeo. 'The ninety-nine-year lease of the plot on which our house stood,' Govindrao continued, 'was due to expire in 1995. Already the family had begun to find the house cramped. A friend of ours who was in the construction business, offered us a flat in an apartment block in Shivaji Park that his company was building. It was a good time to move rather than wait to be forced out in 1995.'

Govindrao and his family—wife Manik, son Amar and daughter Ashwini—moved into their new house, Pushkar, on Dassera day. 'It was also the day that Ashwini gave her first classical music programme. It was on Mumbai Doordarshan's *Kilbil* programme for children which, coincidentally, was being launched the same day.' Ashwini Bhide, later Ashwini Bhide-Deshpande, is one of India's foremost vocalists trained by her mother Manik, a well-known and much-loved guru of the Jaipur–Atrauli gharana.

Although Shivaji Park residents, particularly on the south side, were predominantly Marathi, the neighbourhood was not completely homogeneous. Three Jewish families—the Ruebens, Samsons and Erulkars—lived on the ring roads; my friends Radha Nair and Shantha Warrier lived on Keluskar Road; my schoolmates, the Chauhan siblings, lived near Dadaji Nishant, and my classmate Bhagwan Sherwani lived on Raut Road. Dr Trivikram, a relation of Raja Ravi Varma, lived on the first floor of Radha Kunj on Keluskar Road, next door to Sarah Lodge where the Erulkars lived. He was an impressive old man with a Tagore-like white beard. His son Ajit was my classmate.

Two buildings away from Lalit Estate was a Tamil family whose children Parvati and Vishnu were our playmates. Next door to us was another Tamil family, the Swamis whose children Kamala, Bhalu and Narayan were also our playmates. In the building behind us, now called Jaya Niwas, the ground floor was occupied by four Malayali men who were either single or lived bachelor lives away from their families. The Shahs lived on the first floor. The second floor was occupied by a family of Malabaris. Gopal Menon from this family was the sports reporter for *The Times of India*. The top floor was occupied for a few years by the tall and elegant Mathurs. Mr Mathur was a commercial artist who designed film posters. I remember watching him paint a poster for *Hamari Beti* directed by Shobhana Samarth. The poster featured Samarth at the top and her daughters Nutan and Tanuja, whom she was introducing in the film, below.

Lalit Estate itself was a communal mix. The Raus on the third floor were Chitrapur Saraswats. The Bagalwadikars on the second floor were Kannadigas. The Pereiras on the ground floor were East Indians. Beyond Lalit Estate on the edge of the Churi and Fernandes Wadis was a large one-storeyed building, the ground floor of which was occupied by a noisy municipal school. One part of the first floor was occupied by the Bhatia family comprising the generously proportioned parents and son Anand, and the slim and pretty daughters Pramod and Santosh. Another part was an RSS office which resounded every morning to Sanskrit prayers. My friend Satyadev Dubey, the theatre director, would often drop in there to pay his respects and come over for a breakfast of bread and omelette.

These were Shivaji Park's respectable middle-class families. But the precinct was perhaps home to some who did not quite fit this description. Saadat Hasan Manto, who knew the underbelly of Bombay as no other writer did, has a story called 'Hamid's Baby' set in Shivaji Park. It features a couple of pimps and a commercial sex-worker. The pimp Babu Har Gopal has been asked to treat an out-of-town client Hamid to an evening of pleasure. He takes him around Bombay's red-light district but fails to please him. Hamid is something of a stickler for cleanliness. They comb other streets of the city for hours without success. Finally Babu Har Gopal directs the taxi driver to Shivaji Park, swearing to himself that if Hamid does not like the girl he is about to show him, he will give up pimping forever! The bungalow near the park that he takes Hamid to is sparkling clean and done up in excellent taste. The girl turns out to be a beauty. She wears her sari in the Maharashtrian style made famous in Raja Ravi Varma's paintings. She is seventeen and Hamid is floored. The story ends gorily but that is not pertinent to our purpose. Our purpose is to point to cracks that apparently existed in the middle-class front of the precinct. In those cracks also lived film financiers with shady dealings. We know about them too courtesy of Saadat Hasan Manto.

With few takers for the freehold plots outside the Shivaji Park precinct, the Municipal Corporation provided incentives to its own engineers to invest in them. Many did. For several years thereafter, the area around Dadasaheb Rege Marg was known as Engineers Colony. Few people remember the name now.

7. The Apartment and Modernity

'Western civilization is material, frankly material. It assures progress by the progress of matter—railways, conquest of disease, conquest of the air. These are the triumphs of civilization according to Western measure. No one says, "Now the people are more truthful or more humble".'

—Hind Swaraj, *M.K. Gandhi, 1939*

'Everyone must be his own scavenger. If you become your own bhangi (sweeper), not only will you ensure perfect sanitation for yourself, but you will make your surroundings clean and relieve those whom you call bhangis, of the weight of oppression.'

—The Mind of Mahatma Gandhi,
eds R.K. Prabhu & U.R. Rao, 1945

'As many as 1,370 people have died in India cleaning human excreta. We don't need to romanticize the problem to bring

about change. The basic fact that as human beings we can't have other human beings clean our excreta should lead to the change.'

—Bezwada Wilson speaking at Mallya Aditi International School, Bengaluru, 16 December 2016

WHATEVER THE FATHER OF THE NATION THOUGHT AND said about modernity, the railways and conquest of disease certainly made life easier for the new inhabitants of Shivaji Park. So also the arrival of the flush toilet. Although it took a while for architects to find the appropriate place for toilets in the new apartments they were building, the important thing was that they were hygienic and did away with the inhuman practice of manual scavenging. The railways transported people faster than the trams that still trundled on their north-south routes through the centre of the city. In every way Shivaji Park was moving forward (or in Gandhi's view, morally backward) giving residents a new sense of selfhood. In the old district of Kalbadevi your home was often your workplace and the street was part of your home. In Girgaum your workplace was in the Fort but your home included a convivial veranda and a central courtyard for celebrations and quarrels. In Shivaji Park, your workplace was a long commute away but you had the means to get there rapidly and in comfort. Although your home was contained within the four walls of your block, you had verandas from where to call out to passing vendors of fish and vegetables. And although you did not have common corridors to sit out in and shoot the breeze, you had a 28-acre park—one of the biggest in the city—to relax in, and the sea breeze as bonus.

Dadar West's 'progress of matter' began on 12 April 1867, when the first four-bogey local train left Virar at 6.45 in the morning, picked up passengers from Borivali, Goregaon, Andheri, Bandra, Mahim and Dadar to deposit them at a station in Backbay Reclamation, located somewhere between today's Churchgate and Marine Lines stations. The train left Backbay at 5.30 in the evening to bring passengers home from their workplaces. By 1925, when Shivaji Park came into being, 1,323 trains were running on the Bombay, Baroda and Central India Railway (BB&CI) tracks. Many were electrified and carried around 35 lakh passengers back and forth every day. Long after 1951, when the BB&CI Railway was merged with the Saurashtra, Rajputana, Jaipur State and Cutch State Railways to form the Western Railway, Dadar West station continued to be called BB Dadar and Dadar East GIP Dadar. GIP stood for the Greater Indian Peninsula Railway which had started its local service in 1856.

The railways made another vital aspect of modernity possible. Women were now able to travel unaccompanied to work. Clerks travelled, nurses travelled and teachers travelled by train. Soon there was a visible upswing in the value attached to job-holding women in the lower-middle and middle-middle class marriage market. Modernity for

Marathi women also meant slipping out of the nine-yard kashta lugda into the lighter six-yard sari. Although the nine-yard sari hitched up between the legs had never kept the Marathi woman from cycling, swimming or playing badminton, it announced itself as old fashioned and was seen as unwieldy for women in a hurry.

Another gift of the 'progress of matter' was the flush toilet. For Hindus this was not merely a modern convenience as it was say in England where it was introduced in the mid-19th century, but was fraught with problems. Once the idea of such a toilet was sold to the British people, there were no religio-cultural taboos that they needed to deal with before installing it in their homes. In Shivaji Park the acceptance of the flush toilet as a convenience was one thing, but its placement in the house quite another. Chawl dwellers had not faced any problem regarding toilets whether they were basket privies or flushing toilets. In the early days the basket privies were located safely outside the chawls from where manual scavengers lifted the excreta. Later they were located in the corridors outside the homes, as in the villages and small towns where the residents had come from. In his invaluable book *House But No Garden: Apartment Living in Bombay's Suburbs 1898–1964*, Nikhil Rao gives figures for the gradual shift from basket privies to flushing toilets. The highest number of conversions occurred in 1920–21, over a decade before the Shivaji Park precinct was developed. The problem in Shivaji Park was that there was no place outside the home for toilets. Flats were advertised as self-contained which meant toilets were located inside the flats. But pollution taboos meant they could not be located anywhere in the house. For instance, not next to the kitchen. Caste rules meant that sweepers could not be allowed into the home to clean toilets. There was of course no question of residents cleaning them themselves. The toilets had therefore to be so placed as to allow sweepers to do their job without entering and thus 'polluting' the home.

Architects found two ways of circumventing the problem. In my sister's parents-in-law's flat in Engineers Colony, a narrow corridor separated the bathroom and toilet block from the living areas. The toilet was so placed as to allow the sweeper to enter it using a separate spiral staircase at the back of the building. In Lalit Estate, the bathroom was/is near the kitchen and the toilet beyond it near the front door. The toilet has two doors, one opens into the flat and the other onto the landing. When the sweeper knocks, you open the landing door, so he enters and leaves without entering the house. We used the landing door only when my grandparents lived with us. At all other times it has been kept locked with the sweeper entering the toilet through the house.

Another modern amenity that Shivaji Park residents were privileged to have was piped cooking gas. There was a huge gas meter on the wall of our kitchen and two independent burners on the platform. The gas was supplied by the Bombay Gas Company which had a plant in Parel. The company's main business was providing gas for street lights. Every evening a man would run down the streets of the city, carrying a long pole with a hook at the end which he used to put flame to gas and voila, the lamp was lit. The company halted its operations in 1960. In 1981, the BMC cancelled its licence permanently. Street lights moved from gas to electricity. We had continued to get domestic gas till the mid-'70s when one day, suddenly, our burners would not light. We had received no notice of the supply being turned off. I remember visiting the gas company's office regularly for months to find out where we stood. But absolutely no information was forthcoming. Meanwhile Liquid Petroleum Gas had become available. My mother deeply distrusted the cylinders in which it was packed. She had heard too many stories of their exploding. Also, she had not quite given up hope of the Bombay Gas Company resuming supply. So for years we cooked on kerosene. At last, around 1978, Mother gave up hope and submitted to LPG.

The Shivaji Park apartments offered something else that residents had neither been accustomed to nor demanded: private space. It came as part of the modern design for homes that architects had introduced. Chawls, built for the lower-middle class, were understandably short on space. Each unit consisted of one room, kitchen, mori (a place for washing up) and of course the common corridor. Residents ate, slept and studied in the same room. When sons married, a curtain was hung in the middle of the room to give them a modicum of privacy. But even bungalows of well-off people in the old districts, with their spacious verandas and common family rooms, had very small bedrooms. In the modern apartment, the bedrooms were larger and their number indicated the economic status of the residents. An additional feature of the flats was the never-before-heard thing called the living-cum-dining room. Our flat followed the old bungalow pattern of eating in the kitchen, updated to provide a clearly marked-out space for a dining table. Instead of sitting on the floor as happened in traditional bungalows, we sat at the table. When my grandparents visited from Belgaum, they sat on flat wooden seats between the table and the cooking area, eating off brass plates set on the floor. In all these ways, flats in Shivaji Park became instruments of cultural engineering.

The external design of buildings presented a less fraught expression of modernity. Shivaji Park was happy to be an exemplar of a modern style of architecture that had begun in Europe in the late 1920s and found its most flamboyant expression on South Beach, Miami, Florida. The technological enabler of this style, once called Style Moderne and later Art Deco, was Reinforced Cement Concrete (RCC). The human enablers of the style were architects trained in the Sir J.J. School of Architecture who were in touch with international happenings in the field. They boldly rejected both the vernacular style of architecture and the hybrid Indo-Gothic, Indo-Saracenic forms invented by the colonials, in favour of clean lines, symmetry, graceful curves and stylized decorative motifs on façades. All this was made possible by RCC. An added benefit of the technology for Shivaji Park owners was cost. Building costs had been halved when RCC was first used in the west. Moreover, it had withstood ordeals like fires and earthquakes. Each shock had led to a recognition of the risks involved in using it without full knowledge of its potential and pitfalls. In 1910, the association of cement users in America had published a handbook setting out standard regulations for building with RCC.

Despite this, the technology was first regarded with high suspicion in Bombay. We must admire the confidence shown by Bombay's architects in using it. As it happened, their confidence was fully justified. Not a single building in Shivaji Park collapsed as a five-storey structure in the Churchgate area had done while under construction. Of the many stories one hears about the untiring work that Nanasaheb Modak did in the course of his duties as BMC's chief engineer, one belongs to this crash. He is said to have worked through the night to help rescue victims trapped under the rubble. The widely reported crash happened as late as in the year 1942.

In the early 1970s, greedy developers in Miami, which boasted of some of Art Deco's finest examples, had tried to make a killing there. In 1976, a group of activists got together to found the Miami Design Preservation League. Their fight against the builders' designs ensured that the most striking façades of the precinct were preserved. Mumbai's heritage preservationists have failed to rein in the greed of developers eyeing Shivaji Park properties. Backed by politicians, builders have managed to neutralize their voice. Even the BMC's formally constituted Heritage Committee has had to give way to another avatar, more amenable to the interests of developers. The Shivaji Park residents' interests too have coincided with the builders'. Their homes have been neglected by landlords whose hands have been tied by the Maharashtra Rent Control Act 1999 which began life as Bombay Rents, Hotel and Lodging House Rates Control Act, 1947. The legislation has frozen rents and made tenants' rights of residence practically inviolable. The tenants see redevelopment as the only way to acquire well-maintained homes with the added benefit of ownership. Redevelopment benefits landlords too. Builders pay them large sums of money to relinquish possession of their properties. Builders can afford to do so because they themselves are going to make a killing with the sale of the extra flats left over after tenants have been given theirs. It is a win-win situation all round. The only loser then is heritage and history.

8. Some Eminent People of Shivaji Park

'It was my habit to walk from Portuguese Church to Cadell Road and down to the beach. After walking a couple of lengths there and resting for ten minutes, I would do one round of Shivaji Park. I have not come across any other neighbourhood that offers so many places for a flaneur. There is a cement parapet round Shivaji Park for people to sit on. In the mornings the parapet is alive with groups of people discussing politics. Those who sit near the Gymkhana accompany conversation with tea, coffee, onion bhajjias and misal ordered from its canteen. There is a walking path along the inside of the parapet where again people walk in twos and threes. But I am a loner. I do what you rarely see anyone else in convivial Shivaji Park do. I walk alone.'

—'My Days in Dadar', *Jaywant Dalvi, in*
Bahurangi Bahudhangi Dadar

Shrimati Leela Jog, 30, Shivaji Park, Dadar, Bombay 28

Priya Bhagini,

Aapne rupaye 375 ke cheque ki pahunch bhej di isliye dhanyavad. Aapko rashtrabhasha ka thoda bhi gyan nahi hai kya? Agar woh nahi hai to matrubhasha ka to hoga hi. Dehati auraton ki seva karne ke liye jo bahine taiyar hoti hain, woh angrezi marfat to apna kaam shaayad hi kar saken. Aur main to dehati hun. Usko angrezi mein kyon?

Aapka
Mo. Ka. Gandhi

Dear Sister,

Thank you for acknowledging receipt of the cheque for Rs 375. Have you not even a smattering of the national language? Even if you do not have, surely you know your mother tongue? Sisters who show readiness to serve our rural women can hardly do so in English. And I am but a villager. Why address me in English?

Yours
M.K. Gandhi

—Women Pioneers of Catering Education and Consumer Movement, *Leela Jog, 1994*

THEATRE, MUSIC, FILM, POLITICS, JOURNALISM—ILLUSTRIOUS members from all these fields and their devotees have lived around Shivaji Park. Many of them are now gone. But when they were alive and active, this neighbourhood was one of the most happening in the city.

Jaywant Dalvi was a prolific novelist, playwright and columnist. He worked for many years in the United States Information Centre. One of his jobs was to oversee translations of American books into Marathi. He retired well before reaching superannuation to become a full-time writer. He wrote over two dozen novels, several collections of short fiction and over half-a-dozen plays. He became known nationally for the film he wrote based on his novel *Chakra*. It was directed by Rabindra Dharmaraj who died prematurely soon after it was made. It starred Smita Patil, Naseeruddin Shah and Kulbhushan Kharbanda. Patil won the Filmfare best actress award for her performance. Tragically, she too lived for barely five years after. She died at the age of thirty-one and was cremated at the Shivaji Park crematorium.

Leela Jog had a most unusual life which she has recorded in the book from which the above letter is taken. She had worked for three months in 1945 as Organizing Secretary in the Bombay Office of the Kasturba Gandhi National Memorial Trust. When it closed down, she had still not received her salary. Gandhi's letter is the last in the correspondence that followed.

Leela Jog was the first woman journalist in Bombay to report for a mainline newspaper, *The Bombay Chronicle*. Her husband Narayan Gopal Jog, known as Nana, served on the editorial staff of the paper for several years. He was her first cousin and fourteen years her senior. Leela fell in love with him and they decided to marry. The family was shocked and would have nothing to do with the marriage. Indian law too would not allow it. But there were no laws against marriage between cousins in Ceylon. So they went to Ceylon, got married and returned to live in Nana's flat in Laxmi Nivas, on the north-east corner of Shivaji Park. Leela Jog worked as a 'Ration Girl' in post-war Bombay and became Leelavati Munshi's right hand in providing nutritious food through the Annapoorna Scheme. By a natural progression, she was involved with the team that set up the Catering College. Finally she worked with the Consumer Guidance Society of India.

Saurab Rao

Laxmi Nivas, home to Leela and Nana Jog

Nana Jog was popular for his weekly *Bombay Chronicle* column 'Occasional Comments'. After six years with the paper, both he and his close colleague K.A. Abbas, also a

Shivaji Park resident quit—Abbas to join *Blitz* and Jog to join *The Sunday Standard* as editor. Later he took over as editor of *The Indian Express*. But more than his journalism, it was his book *Judge or Judas* (1945) that made him widely known. The book was a strong response to *Verdict on India* (1944) written by British playwright-novelist-actor Beverley Nichols. A reviewer had said about Nichols' views that they were 'lively and quite amusing to start with, but they deteriorate, degenerate even, to condemn and deride all things Indian, religion, culture, people, music, politics. His verdict is "Guilty"!'

The stretch of Keluskar Road North that leads from Savarkar Marg to the beach was once home to a number of eminent people. Premnath and Bina Rai lived in a building at the seaside end. Sadashiv J. Row Kavi and Prahlad Keshav Atre lived in a building midway down the road. Row Kavi was the producer-director of films like *Begaana*, *Didi* and *Bhabhi ki Chudiyan.* His son Ashok Row Kavi was a journalist till 1990, when he founded *Bombay Dost*, India's first LGBT publication. He is the founder-chairperson of the Humsafar Trust, which was active in the agitation for decriminalizing homosexuality in India. 6 September 2018 saw the triumphant end of the battle, when a bench of the Chief Justice of India Dipak Misra and Justices Rohinton Nariman, A.M. Khanwilkar, D.Y. Chandrachud and Indu Malhotra legalized same-sex relations between consenting adults in a unanimous judgement.

For Pralhad Keshav Atre, educationist, journalist, playwright, film-maker and author, the greatest attraction of Shivaji Park was the proximity of the sea. 'The sea is my companion in Mumbai,' he writes in the first of his four memoirs. 'The murmur of its waves through night and day, fills my life like a background score. My spirits lift and dance to the beat of its tides. I quaff the crazy breeze and sway intoxicated like the tall palms that line the beach. What poetry there is in walking unshod on crisp, wet sand at break of day with droplets from the crashing waves spraying the body! When I see people walking on the beach, their bodies sealed tight in clothes, I want to ask, "Why don't you let God's holy water touch your skins? Let His air blow freely into your noses and eyes. As in any other temple, footwear is to be left outside in Nature's temple too."'

Atre was a large man with a matching voice. His oratorical and writing skills had won him an enormous following. Popularly known as Acharya Atre, he was the founder-editor of the mainline daily *Maratha*. His film, *Shyamchi Aai*, won the award for best film at India's first National Film Awards held in 1954. The book on which the film was based also bore the same title. Written by author, teacher, social activist and freedom fighter Pandurang Sadashiv Sane (Sane Guruji), *Shyamchi Aai* is a collection of autobiographical tales about how his mother's upbringing taught him all that he practised in life. Atre's other notable film, *Mahatma Phule*, won the President's Silver Medal. Atre wrote seven plays, many of them adapted from European sources. His version of Brandon Thomas's *Charlie's Aunt* as *Moruchi Mavshi* was re-adapted in 1998 to the Hindi screen as *Aunty No. 1*, starring Govinda and Raveena Tandon.

However, even before Atre became a playwright, journalist, editor and film director, he had been an educationist. Returning to India with a Diploma in Teaching from London, he was disappointed to see the dry-as-dust textbooks which were being used to teach schoolchildren Marathi. So he wrote two series of readers for primary and secondary schoolchildren—*Navayug Vachanmala* and *Arun Vachanmala*—to make them understand and love the language. So varied were the selections of prose and poetry in the readers and so lively the writing style, that entire generations in Maharashtra swear even today that they owe their love for the language to the two vachanmalas.

At the other end of the road from Row Kavi and Atre lived C. Ramchandra, the much-loved music director. He was a man of many parts, for each of which he had a different name. Born Ramchandra Narhar Chitalkar, he was C. Ramachandra as music director, R.N. Chitalkar as actor and simply Chitalkar as an occasional playback singer. Many of the songs he sang became hits, like his duet with Lata Mangeshkar, '*Kitna haseen hai mausam*' from *Azad* and '*Shola jo bhadke*' from *Albela*. His most timeless songs were scored for the Bina Rai-Pradeep Kumar starrer *Anarkali*. He also composed the ultimate patriotic song, Kavi Pradeep's

'*Ae mere watan ke logon*', heart-rendingly sung by Lata Mangeshkar. A sophisticated musician of his caliber did not deserve the rather unimaginative memorial erected to him on 25 April 1999. It stands outside the Scouts Pavilion across the chowk named after him, comprising a faux wooden plaque with his name and an ottava symbol on top.

An equally crude memorial has been erected at the other end of Shivaji Park in memory of another fine music composer, Vasant Desai, who lived and died in Parimal located there. Inscribed with his name, it shows a disembodied arm rising out of the pedestal holding up a veena. Vasant Desai composed memorable songs, basing many of them on Hindustani ragas. He discovered Vani Jairam who sang the Malhar-based '*Bol re papihara*' for *Guddi*, Jaya Bhaduri's first film. He also persuaded Ustad Amir Khan to sing the vigorous Adana-based '*Jhanak jhanak payal baaje*' for V. Shantaram's film of the same name. With the Bhairav-based '*Ae malik tere bande hum*' in *Do Aankhen Bara Hath*, he made devotion sublimely melodious.

Pandit Jawaharlal Nehru was once reported to have remarked regretfully that Indian schoolchildren seemed unable to sing '*Jana Gana Mana*' tunefully in one voice. He believed that if they could do that, it would automatically instill in them the twin ideals of unity and patriotism. The then education minister of Maharashtra took the idea seriously. He requested Vasant Desai to see what could be done about it. Desai ran workshops for teachers, recorded appropriate songs for children and travelled all over the state to teach students of primary schools how to sing them. He called this programme *Ek sur, ek taal.* As a result, when Nehru addressed a meeting in Shivaji Park sometime later, Desai was able to present before him a chorus of thousands of schoolchildren singing the national anthem in unison and in tune. In memory of the musical bond Desai had formed with schoolchildren, a children's concert is held at the memorial every year on 22 December, the day Desai died in a tragic accident at his home. Once a Shivaji Park resident, Somnath Parab, a singer and disciple of Vasant Desai, leads the concert under the auspices of his organization Yuva Kala Manch. On this day groups of schoolchildren from across the city sing the works of saints, poets and lyricists. Hearing their pure voices ring through the morning air in perfect tune is a moving experience.

Parimal, where Vasant Desai lived, was also home to Prakash Mohadikar, an ardent follower of Sane Guruji in whose name he founded Sane Guruji Vidyalaya, located in the erstwhile Fernandes Wadi down the road from us. Mohadikar, fondly called Prakashbhai, had to quit his job as a teacher at Dadar's Chhabildas School because he had called for a strike to mourn Subhas Chandra Bose's death. When Sane Guruji died in 1950, he decided to dedicate his life to spreading his teachings. 'There is but one dharma', goes one of Sane Guruji's most well-known songs, 'And that is to offer love to the world'. Prakashbhai's urge to serve society, particularly the disadvantaged, led to his starting a night school for domestic workers in Sane Guruji Vidyalaya. Hundreds of boys who, driven by poverty, had left their villages to take up domestic work in the city, went to the night school after work to equip themselves for better employment prospects.

Improbably, in the same building as our patriotic music composer Vasant Desai and the saint-like Prakashbhai, lived P.N Arora, producer-director of a series of forgettable 'B' grade films. With him lived the gorgeous queen of the 'cabaret', Helen. Not once in the seventeen years that she lived with Arora, did the residents of Shivaji Park suspect that she was being ruthlessly exploited by him financially and otherwise. When she finally escaped his clutches, with a little help from Salim, one half of the Salim-Javed team of script and dialogue writers, she was virtually penniless. She had to fight a longdrawn court case to reclaim some of her money.

There were a couple of large studios in Dadar which attracted film people to the neighbourhood. Comedian Gope lived on Raut Road North. His pairing with Yakub made them India's version of Laurel and Hardy. Kishore Sahu who directed *Kunwara Baap* and *Nadiya ke Paar* and was briefly married to actor Snehaprabha Pradhan lived on Cadell Road. Master Vinayak, who had introduced the young Lata Mangeshkar in his Marathi film *Pahili Manglagaur*, lived in Suman Niwas on Keluskar Road North.

Baby Nanda was his daughter. Shahu Modak, famous for playing Krishna and other mythological characters in Hindi films, is commemorated with a chowk on Cadell Road.

As film studios moved northward from Dadar, so did film people. G.R. Kamat, the unassuming screenplay writer, who wrote most of Raj Khosla's hit films between 1957 and 1983, continued to live in his modest middle-class flat on Lt Dilip Gupte Marg which cuts through Keluskar and Raut Roads North and bears the mixed-identity postal description of 'Shivaji Park, Mahim West, Dadar'. He wrote *Bambai ka Babu*, *Kala Pani*, *Do Badan*, *Mera Saya*, *Do Raste, Do Chor*, *Mera Gaon Mera Desh*, *Kachhe Dhage*, *Do Premee*, *Basera* and *Pukar*. He was associate screenwriter with G.D. Madgulkar for the hit Marathi film *Lakhachi Gosht* which introduced two young sister-actors Kumud and Kusum Sukhtankar, as Rekha and Chitra. Kamat married Rekha. A regular walker around Shivaji Park, Kamat was ninety-two when he died on 6 October 2015.

Shivaji Park's most recent showbiz resident is 'bhajan samrat' Anup Jalota who lives in Mohan Niwas on Keluskar Road. All in all one might say Shivaji Park was Pali Hill and Juhu before they became hosts to glamour.

If C. Ramchandra and Vasant Desai represented the best in Hindi film music, three glittering gems represented the best in Hindustani music—Pandit Sharadchandra Arolkar, Pandit Jasraj and Surashree Kesarbai Kerkar. Pt Arolkar, popularly known as buwa, was, after the gharana patriarch

Pandit Krishnarao Shankar Pandit, the most eminent exponent of the Gwalior gharana. He lived in Usha on Raut Road. Gaunt and ascetic, his music was not made to win the hearts of large audiences at music conferences. He was at his best in private mehfils where he could share the striking beauties of his gayaki with knowledgeable rasikas. He described music as fluid sculpture. One saw the description reflected in his music, its effect being both playful and spiritual. Poet Dilip Chitre, one of Arolkar's most knowledgeable and ardent admirers, once described Pt Krishnarao Shankar Pandit as the warrior and Pt Sharadchandra Arolkar as the yogi of the Gwalior gharana. In an article in *The Economic Times* dated 16 April 1989, the venerable music critic Mohan Nadkarni described the effect of a Yaman that Pt Arolkar had sung in a concert at Sane Guruji Vidyalaya, as 'a musical piece that will long linger in my memory. Without exaggeration, it came to us as an impassioned utterance of a deeply moved soul. He sang it in an exalted strain, in which every note, every phrase, every pattern came as an act of consecration.'

Pt Arolkar was a difficult man, as much for himself as for his disciples. In her book on him and his music, Neela Bhagwat, one of his seniormost disciples, writes in a chapter headed '*Ek Ashant Kalakar*' (An unquiet artist): 'Buwa's nature was our fate. His subtle music and musical thought, our fortune.' Pt Arolkar died on 4 June 1994, at the age of eighty-two.

Pandit Jasraj, veteran vocalist of the Mewati gharana who made Haveli sangeet popular on the concert stage, lives in the corner house at the north-east end of Shivaji Park with his wife Madhura, V. Shantaram's daughter by his first wife. While V. Shantaram needed nobody's permission to marry his second wife, actor Jayashree and his third wife, actor Sandhya, he put Pt Jasraj through some tough tests before permitting him to marry his daughter. Jasraj has innovated a unique form of jugalbandi which he calls Jasrangi, in which a male and a female singer sing different raags in their respective scales to create a single piece of music.

Beyond the bend in the road from Pt Jasraj's house down Lt Dilip Gupte Marg lived Kesarbai Kerkar, imperious inheritor of the Jaipur-Atrauli gharana and its crown jewel. G.N. Joshi, himself a musician of no mean achievement, once invited her to record for the Indian Gramophone Company, popularly known as HMV, for which he worked. She came, recorded and was about to leave when Joshi apologetically asked her to repeat the performance. The recording equipment had sprung a glitch. 'Your equipment failed. Not mine,' she said and walked out.

Sitarist Pt Shankar Abhyankar, who has a fund of stories about music and musicians, once told me that Kesarbai Kerkar used to carry a list of names of people she did not want at her concerts. Organizers were responsible for keeping them out. Her granddaughter Ila justifies this in Namita Devidayal's book *The Music Room*, 'Her music was her wealth. Don't you lock up your jewellery in a safe and bring it out only for special occasions or people?' The persona non grata on Kesarbai's list were kept out because they stole her music and sang it in shamefully crude ways.

Kesarbai was a perfectionist. Pt Abhyankar has a story about the last concert he heard. It was at the Aptes' bungalow at Kemps Corner. The bungalow was going to be demolished and the industrialist family wanted to fill it with music before it fell. Music connoisseur, humorist, film-maker and actor-director P.L. Deshpande was the Master of Ceremonies. After the concert, Kesarbai told him she would stop singing once she had honoured the commitments she had already made. Taken aback, Deshpande protested. 'My voice has grown old,' she said. 'Not at all. This was a brilliant concert,' Deshpande countered. 'Perhaps you didn't notice it,' she said; 'but my voice shook a couple of times.' True to her word, she did not sing a single note for the remaining twelve years of her life. But her voice, singing the incomparable Bhairavi composition, '*Jaat kahaan ho*' is included on the 12-inch gold-plated copper disc *Sounds of Earth*, that has been travelling through outer space billions of miles from the earth on Voyager 1 since 2012.

Kesarbai died on 16 September 1977 at the age of eighty-five. One of Marathi's finest poets, Sadanand Rege was moved to dedicate a poem to her which ended, 'I am but a deaf man / But one who / Blinded by the beauty / Of your song / Sings his blindness.'

A chowk at the north-east end of Shivaji Park is named after poet Raja Badhe. His lyrics, sung by the foremost singers of the 1960s and '70s, made him popular in Maharashtra. When V.D. Savarkar, a poet besides being the father of Hindutva, was asked to write the lyrics for Vijay Bhatt's film *Ramrajya*, he pointed to Raja Badhe as the right man for the job. Badhe's most significant literary contribution was his translation into modern Marathi of *Gatha Saptashati*, a 5th-century collection of 700 single verse poems about love in all its aspects, written in the ancient Maharashtri language. The translation was published by the Maharashtra State Government. Raja Badhe's brother Babanrao, who lives on the north-west side of Shivaji Park, sheds an interesting light on Rajabhau's early years in Bombay. In a long article sent to Jayant Kulkarni, inveterate collector of stories about Shivaji Park and its people, he says that Rajabhau once shared a ground-floor flat on Cadell Road near the crematorium with Mahesh Kaul, Kishore Sahu and Amritlal Nagar. They were strugglers then. Later Rajabhau established himself as a lyricist and Mahesh Kaul went on to make the hit film *Naujawan*, remembered even today for the song '*Thandi hawaen lehrake aayen*' composed by S.D. Burman and sung by Lata Mangeshkar. Kishore Sahu became a successful film writer-actor-director and Pandit Amritlal Nagar, a screenplay writer, before he turned to writing fiction and became one of the most powerful voices in Hindi literature.

G.D. Madgulkar was another illustrious Marathi poet who spent a few years in Shivaji Park. His magnum opus, the *Geet Ramayana*, is a retelling of the epic in modern verse. Sudhir Phadke, who lived in Shankar Niwas on Dadasaheb Rege Marg, gave music and voice to the lyrics, composing them in ragas that suited the time of day and season when the concerned episodes were taking place. *Geet Ramayana* was broadcast over All India Radio, Pune, one episode at a time every week for a whole year, holding Maharashtra in thrall. It has been translated into nine languages with five versions in Hindi alone.

Dadar was and continues to be awash with a passion for music, both classical and film. Anil Nagarkar, who lives in a building facing Shivaji Park south, runs an organization called Sargam, devoted to old film songs. He hosts monthly meetings where like-minded people gather to listen to cherished recordings. Jayant Kulkarni reports a meeting with Dr Atul Kaji, Kesarbai Kerkar's grandson who, like Kulkarni, is a passionate devotee of old Hindi film songs. In the course of the meeting, Kaji challenged Kulkarni for going on and on about Lata Mangeshkar. He then proceeded to sing song after song of old greats like Kanan Devi, Shamshad Begum, Johrabai, Lalita Deulkar, Geeta Dutt, Suraiya, Sulochana Chavan-Kadam, Meena Kapur, Sudha Malhotra, Suman Kalyanpur, K.L. Saigal, Pankaj Mullick, Jagmohan Sursagar, Hemant Kumar, Mohammed Rafi and Talat Mahmood. 'Then he did something that made my jaw drop,' says Kulkarni. 'He brought out his collection of old 78 RPMs along with his Garrard Record Changer. Beginning with playing Kanan Devi's "*Ae chand chhupna jaana*", he ended with Pankaj Mullick's "*Aai bahar aaj aai bahar*". I don't know how three hours flew by. As a finale Atul played "*Jalke dil khak hua*", Lata's song from *Parichay*. "There you are," I said. "You had to come back to Lata." To which Atul said, "Jayu, finally, Lata is Lata."'

The Kamerkars, a large theatre family, lived a short walk away from my house on Ranade Road. Their biggest contribution to theatre, film and television was Sulabha Deshpande, married to actor-director Arvind Deshpande. In the '60s, the experimental theatre movement in Mumbai had been spearheaded by Vijaya Mehta (née Jayawant) in Marathi and Satyadev Dubey in Hindi. The Deshpandes had been members of Mehta's group Rangayan. When the group split, they along with their colleague Arun Kakade founded the theatre group Awishkar and continued the movement in the Chhabildas Boys High School near Dadar station where Sulabha Deshpande was a teacher. The school hall up three flights of rickety stairs was the centre of a vibrant multi-lingual theatre movement from the early '70s to the late '80s. It died a predictable death when the economy was liberalized and money became the dominant value in every field, including culture.

The plays at Chhabildas had offered an alternative to the mainstream plays staged at Shivaji Mandir on N.C. Kelkar

Road. Before the 1992-93 post Babri Masjid demolition riots, it was often booked for three shows every day: 11 in the morning, 4 in the afternoon and 7.30 in the evening. After the riots, the 7.30 shows dried up because people were reluctant to go out at night. This reluctance increased with the coming of satellite television around 1995. Further, as old buildings began to be redeveloped, the Marathi residents of Shivaji Park began moving out to the northern suburbs and Marathi theatre moved with them. Soon the 11 a.m. shows in Shivaji Mandir also stopped. Today most of its shows are staged at four o'clock in the afternoon.

Once cricketers were the stars of Shivaji Park. Manohar Hardikar, Ramakant Desai, Subhash and Baloo Gupte, Sandeep Patil, Ajit Wadekar, Vijay Manjrekar, Bapu Nadkarni all lived here. Although Madhav and Arvind Apte lived elsewhere, they played here. The star among stars, Sachin Tendulkar and his friend Vinod Kambli, both classmates at Dadar's Sharadashram School, trained here under the revered cricket guru, winner of the Dronacharya award, Ramakant Achrekar.

The cricketing history of Shivaji Park has been recorded by many. So we shall not dwell on it here, but pass on to Shivaji Park's industrialist family, the Camlin Dandekars. The Camlin Art Contest for schoolchildren was one of the most looked-forward-to events in the '70s. With almost 50 lakh students from across the country participating, it simply walked into the Guinness World Records. The Dandekar brothers D.P. and G.P. had begun their business with ink. They made it in a vat in their single room in Girgaum and called it Horse Brand Ink. As their business diversified into fountain pens, they were strapped for space and moved to Shivaji Park to a house on D.V. Deshpande Marg, behind Udyam. They now began looking for a catchier name. It came to D.P. Dandekar in the unlikeliest of places: an Irani restaurant. This is how it happened, he says in his book *Untavarcha Pravas* (Journey on a Camel). He was sitting with a friend sipping tea when he noticed an advertisement for Camel cigarettes. He began linking ideas absently: camel, hump, storing nourishment, walking for miles without running out. Fountain pens, storing ink, miles of writing without running out. Eureka. There was the name. Camel. With it came the portmanteau name Camlin, a brand that became synonymous with schoolchildren's stationery needs. Later, the Dandekars diversified further into paints and art materials.

For many decades, politicians and Shivaji Park went together. Today we have only Raj Thackeray of the Maharashtra Navnirman Sena facing the park and Manohar Joshi, superannuated by the Shiv Sena, near Dadar beach.

Of all the politicians who lived here, the one who stood head and shoulders above everyone else for his probity in public life was Madhu Dandavate, minister for railways in the Morarji Desai government and finance minister in the V.P. Singh cabinet. When Dandavate died in November

2005, Singh said, 'Even in death he served the country and mankind by donating his body.' As minister for railways, he campaigned vigorously for the Konkan Railway and is considered one of its founders.

Writing a tribute in *The Hindu Magazine* after Dandavate's death on 12 November 2005, historian Ramachandra Guha said, 'Dandavate first introduced the computerisation of railway reservations, an innovation that greatly reduced corruption and made life less intolerable for commuters. Dandavate's second innovation was more far-reaching still. This was to put two inches of foam on what passed for "reserved sleeper berths" in the second-class sections of trains. When introducing the change, Dandavate said, "What I want to do is not degrade the first class, but elevate the second class".

'In February 1979, I was in Ahmedabad, visiting a friend at the National Institute of Design (NID). I went to the railway station to buy my return ticket to Delhi; also in the queue, and a few places behind me, was my friend's NID classmate, who happened to be the son of the Railway Minister. This was characteristic, not just of this particular family, but of their political tradition as a whole. The sons and daughters of the Maharashtra socialists never took advantage of their parents' political position; and always followed a career different from theirs.

'Twelve years after standing ahead of Uday Dandavate in a railway queue, I met his father for the first and last time. I was at the Delhi airport, waiting for my wife. Her flight was delayed. While I waited, a succession of politicians passed by. A General Election was around the corner, so naturally there was much high-powered traffic to the capital from the mofussil. I saw N.T. Rama Rao and N.D. Tewari come and go, each met by a set of grovelling minions. Then came Dandavate, who was met by no one. He simply picked up his suitcase from the belt and walked out with it.'

At the other end from Dandavate in every way is Manohar Joshi, chief minister of Maharashtra from 1995 to 1999, minister of heavy industries in the Atal Bihari Vajpayee government from 1999 to 2002, speaker of the Lok Sabha from 2002 to 2004, Rajya Sabha member from 2006 to 2010. He lives in an apartment on Keluskar Road South, close to the crematorium.

The Srikrishna Commission Report on the Mumbai riots of 1992–93 held Joshi and his mentor Bal Thackeray responsible for inciting Shiv Sainiks to violence. As chief minister, Joshi termed the report 'anti-Hindu, pro-Muslim and biased' and refused to adopt the commission's recommendations. Later, he had to resign from the chief ministership when he was held guilty by the Supreme Court of favouring his son-in-law in a land deal in Pune. He himself is in the real estate business. He has gone on record saying making money was always his first goal. Politics and construction are two assured ways of making it. However, he had to quit politics when Shiv Sainiks booed him off the stage at Shivaji Park on 13 October 2013 at the party's most important annual event, the Dussehra rally. He was thought to have been hobnobbing with Sharad Pawar. This was seen as his attempt at keeping his political options open in case his clout in the Shiv Sena continued to wane. Shiv Sainiks even stoned his house in 2014 before the general elections.

Vinayak Damodar Savarkar, writer, revolutionary of the Independence struggle, creator of the word Hindutva and founder of the Hindu Mahasabha, lived on Dr M.B. Raut Road in the three-storey Savarkar Sadan of which only one-third now remains with the family. The building cannot be redeveloped because of its heritage status.

Savarkar's poem, made famous by the Mangeshkar family's rendition of it, expressed his emotional state while he was incarcerated in the Cellular Jail in the Andamans for his revolutionary activities. The poem begins '*Ne majasi ne parat matrubhumila / Sagara pran talamalala.*' (Take me back to my motherland / Oh ocean, my being is in agony.) His other well-known poem, 'Jayostute', sung by Lata Mangeshkar is written in heavily Sankritized Marathi in praise of the Motherland. The title Swatantryaveer (Warrior of Independence) was conferred on Savarkar by his followers for his early involvement in revolutionary politics. Narendra Modi, our current prime minister, is said to be his ardent admirer. Amrita Shah informs us in her excellent book, *Ahmedabad*, that a small black statue of Savarkar stands outside the city's cultural centre, Sanskar Kendra. There is a full seated one on the terrace of the Savarkar Rastriya Smarak at Shivaji Park. It depicts him dressed in a dhoti and black cap, holding an umbrella in one hand and pointing at the sky with the index finger of the other. A portrait of Savarkar was unveiled in the Central Hall of Parliament in February 2003, when the first NDA government led by Atal Bihari Vajpayee was in power. With all that, Savarkar has also been a controversial figure. One, his several mercy pleas to the British for release from the Cellular Jail and his acceptance of the condition, that he would stop all political activity if released, have been questioned. Two, despite his having been acquitted of involvement in M.K. Gandhi's assassination, the suspicion that he was involved has stuck. He died on 26 February 1966 after giving up food, drink and medication. He said it was time for atmasamarpan (surrendering of the self) when one had completed the mission one was born for.

Another political activist who lived in Shivaji Park, for which reason his statue stands in the middle of the traffic island opposite Udyam, was Pandurang Mahadev Bapat. He is known as Senapati for his leadership of the Mulshi Dam agitation by farm tenants against a dam to be constructed on the Mula river in Pune district by the Tatas. The compensation money, when it was finally paid, went to the landlords, not to the tillers of the lands who had agitated.

Bapat began his political activism as a revolutionary in London where he had gone to study for a degree in

Swapnil Bhole

The great warrior Senapati Bapat with City Engineer N.V. Modak's bungalow, Udyam, in the background

engineering. He learned bomb-making there. He met the Savarkar brothers, Vinayak and Ganesh, who were also in London and planning to blow up the Houses of Parliament. The plan fell through. Back in India, Bapat was involved in the Alipore bomb case and went into hiding.* During his days underground, he discovered that the larger majority of Indians had no idea that the country was under foreign rule. So he gave up revolutionary activities and started educating the public on what it meant to be slaves. He was

*Colloquially referred to as the Alipore Bomb Case, the Muraripukur conspiracy, or the Manicktolla bomb conspiracy, was a criminal case held in India in 1908. The case saw the trial of a number of Indian nationalists of the Anushilan Samiti in Calcutta, under charges of 'waging war against the Government' of the British Raj.

jailed for three years for the Alipore bomb case after which he aligned himself with Bal Gangadhar Tilak's movement to create local organizations to support the cause of Indian Independence. In his last political shift, he became a subscriber to Gandhiji's vision of Swaraj. The Mulshi Dam satyagraha, which came after this shift, saw Bapat back in jail for vandalizing the construction project. He was not arrested. He turned himself in. He was jailed a third time for addressing a public rally held by Subhas Chandra Bose. For these diverse activities in the cause of the country's freedom, Bapat was granted the honour of hoisting the national flag in Pune on 15 August 1947. His last battle was fought from 1955 to 1960 for a united Maharashtra. The statue in the middle of the traffic island opposite Udyam at Shivaji Park was inaugurated by finance minister Yeshwantrao Chavan on 29 November 1970. It shows a frail old man in a dhoti pointing towards Dadar Chowpatty. It totally belies the eventful trajectory of his political life. He died on 28 November 1967. The government of India issued a commemorative stamp in his honour on his tenth death anniversary.

Then there was the Congressman, Prabhakar Kashinath Kunte, a regular Shivaji Park morning walker. He won as many elections to the Maharashtra State Legislative Assembly as he lost. He lost the Vile Parle seat in 1987 to Dr Ramesh Y. Prabhoo of the Shiv Sena. The Shiv Sena chief Bal Thackeray had put his all into the campaign, fighting it on the Hindutva plank. Kunte filed a petition in the Bombay High Court accusing Prabhoo of seeking votes on religious grounds which amounted to an electoral malpractice. Justice S.P. Bharucha declared Prabhoo's election void. However, Prabhoo appealed to the Supreme Court. By the time its judgement supporting the Bombay High Court came, Prabhoo had served out his term. Kunte was finally vindicated in 1996 with a landmark judgment that debarred Thackeray from contesting the elections or voting in them for a period of six years. Kunte died on 15 August 2012 at the age of eighty-nine.

Bal Thackeray grew up and lived in Shivaji Park for many years before he moved to Matoshree in Kala Nagar, Bandra East. His Shivaji Park home was in a small lane off Ranade Road, a few hundred metres from the Bapat statue. His politics and political activities are too well-known to need documentation here. Raj Thackeray, his nephew, disappointed at not having been named Balasaheb's successor, quit the Shiv Sena in January 2006. He founded a new party, the Maharashtra Navnirman Sena (MNS) two months later on 9 March. He began promisingly enough, appearing to have a truly new idea for Maharashtra. One of his first programmes was an exhibition of books in Shivaji Park. Political parties are not known for promoting reading and thinking in their constituencies. And yet, here were tables and tables of books of every shade of social and political thought. But that turned out to be a one-off programme. The back rooms of the exhibition shamiana, which had displayed weapons from Shivaji's times, soon took centre stage pushing books and reading into the background. The MNS was in business, roughing up 'outsiders' for taking away jobs from the sons of the soil.

9. Samyukta Maharashtra

The Battle for a State

'The report of the State Reorganisation Commission was published on October 10, 1955. Much good and bad has happened in Maharasthra in the course of its history. But one can only admire with a full heart the persistence with which the bahujans or common people of Maharashtra pursued the cause of a Consolidated Maharashtra. We saw then the powerful bonds that tied every man and woman out there to unbounded pride in Maharashtra. Leaders of every political stripe worked with a single aim in mind—that the agitation for the State should not take any untoward turn. It was important to channel the resistance of the people towards the disciplined and peaceful employment of satyagraha. That is why the Samyukta Maharashtra Samiti began a peaceful agitation.'

'The Congress Party, which had received overwhelming support from voters in Maharashtra in the 1952 elections, suffered a total rout at their hands in the 1957 elections. In that election voters shared a single faith—faith in the creation of Maharashtra State. They paid no heed to any other value. They turned their backs on the infinite respect in which they held Nehru, a leader of international stature; on the prestige of the tallest leaders of the land; on caste bonds and on pride in religion.'

—From Navya Maharashtrache Bhavitavya *(The Future of the New Maharashtra), G.B. Sardar in* Maharashtra Jeevan, *Vol 2, ed. G.B. Sardar, pub Messrs Joshi and Lokhande Prakashan, 1960*

SHIVAJI PARK BECAME THE BATTLEGROUND FOR THE Samyukta Maharashtra Chalwal, launched in 1955 with the slogan '*Mumbai, Belgaon, Nipani, Karwar, Daman-sah Samyukta Maharashtra Jhalach Pahije*' (A consolidated state of Maharashtra, including Mumbai, Belgaum, Nipani, Karwar and Daman must happen). The fight was against the bilingual state of Maharashtra and Gujarat that had been proposed in the State Reorganisation Commission (SRC) report. For five years, till the battle was won, Shivaji Park rang with the voices of Maharashtra's tallest leaders from the Left, Right and Centre, exhorting people to fight till victory was won.

The Indian government feared that creating linguistic states would lead to linguistic fanaticism and the balkanization of the newly united nation. Govind Ballabh Pant stated in a Parliamentary debate that Gujaratis and Maharashtrians complemented and supplemented each other's qualities. Maharashtrians had more valour, and Gujaratis more discretion, he said. The Lok Sabha debates culminated in a decision to modify the original SRC proposal only to the extent that Vidarbha, which had been awarded independent Statehood in the report, would now be included in Bombay State which would continue to be bilingual. Regarding Bombay, the major bone of contention, the cabinet had decided to make it a union territory for five years with the proviso that a final decision about its status would be taken at the end of the period.

In the Lok Sabha debate on 15 November 1955, the Congressman S.K. Patil had proposed that Bombay be made an autonomous city-state, arguing that this would ensure it retained its cosmopolitan character. Patil was vilified for his stand and became the most reviled Congressman in Bombay's history. In his glory days he had been elected mayor of Bombay three times in a row, earning the title of 'the uncrowned king of Bombay'. In the 1967 election, he lost his seat to the thirty-seven-year-old firebrand Samyukta Socialist Party leader and trade unionist George Fernandes. The victory earned Fernandes the title of 'George the giant-killer'.

The Congressmen of Maharashtra were trapped between their loyalty to the Party line and their natural instinct to align themselves with their linguistic brothers. They stood dithering on the sidelines throughout the battle, giving weak assurances of ultimate justice. The other parties disbelieved them and formed the Samyukta Maharashtra Samiti on 6 February 1956. Bal Thackeray's father Keshav Sitaram Thackeray used his diplomatic and leadership skills to bring the assorted parties together under one umbrella. The Samiti planned to use satyagraha, a non-violent agitation, to achieve their purpose. However, violence did happen, much of it unleashed by the state. Thousands of agitators were lathi-charged and arrested during the five years of the struggle. Thackeray senior was one of those arrested.

The incident that remains carved in the memories of the people of Maharashtra was the brutal shooting of 105 demonstrators at Flora Fountain on 21 November 1955 at the behest of Morarji Desai, the then chief minister of Bombay State. After Maharashtra State was formed on 1 May 1960, with Bombay as its capital, Flora Fountain was renamed Hutatma Chowk in honour of the martyrs who had died there that day. At the time, Bal Thackeray was the staff cartoonist in *The Free Press Journal*; but he was also moonlighting for P.K. Atre's periodical *Navayug*. He commemorated the day of the firing with a cartoon titled Narbhakshak (maneater), which showed Morarji Desai sitting on top of a pile of corpses declaring, 'I am a pure vegetarian'. As a result of his aggressive action of

21 November, Desai was removed from the chief ministership and replaced by Yashwantrao Chavan.

It is possible that 105 was the number of deaths by shooting that occurred in different places in Maharashtra at various times. Newspaper reports were not unanimous in putting the number of dead at Flora Fountain at 105. There is also a counter story to the claims that agitators were always peaceful. A *Time* magazine report dated 30 January 1956 says: 'The rioters blocked streets with boulders and gasoline drums, tore up lamp-posts, ripped down fences. They smashed statues of Mahatma Gandhi (a Gujarati himself), burned Desai in effigy, flourished pictures of Nehru hung with old shoes as a gesture of despisal. Mobs, sometimes 10,000 strong, stormed police stations, looted Gujarati shops, flung electric light bulbs filled with nitric acid in the faces of police and passersby. Saboteurs derailed trains, hurled stones at buses, set fire to cars.'

This too could be a partial view of the five years of agitation. However, where Gandhi himself had found it difficult to ensure a totally peaceful battle for India's Independence, it is entirely likely that the leaders of the Samyukta Maharashtra movement were not always successful in ensuring a peaceful agitation.

P.K. Atre was one of the most charismatic leaders of the movement. His editorials along with Thackeray's cartoons made *Navayug* a veritable mouthpiece of the struggle. His speeches in Shivaji Park—published as a collection titled

Jhalach Pahije (Must happen)—were attended by thousands of people. He made one of his most famous speeches after Nehru's meeting at Girgaum Chowpatty on 3 June 1956 in which he had declared his cabinet's decision to make Bombay a union territory for the next five years. He had also stated that he would not buckle under the Samyukta Maharashtra Samiti's 'hooliganism'.

A week later, on 10 June, Atre addressed a rally of some two lakh people at Shivaji Park. I reproduce below part of the speech in my translation to give the reader some idea of his oratorical skills and the response from the crowd, which is included in the published speech:

'Honourable chairman, brothers and sisters [The audience roars: "United Maharashtra with Belgaum and Mumbai must happen!"] Yes. That is our demand. But Nehru refuses to agree. For the last nine months the three crore strong Marathi public has been shouting in one voice that we want Mumbai. We want Nipani. The thirty-three crore gods in heaven must have heard us shout, but we have failed to enter the ears and hearts of the Congressmen ruling Delhi. Last Sunday, Pandit Nehru turned all our dreams to dust. In a supposedly enormous rally made up of some twenty-five thousand Gujaratis and policemen [loud laughter] he declared that Mumbai will not be ours for five years.

'Nehru says Mumbai will not be ours for five years. Sadoba [S.K. Patil] says it will not be ours for another five thousand years. The difference of three zeroes between the two men's predictions is equal to the difference in their human worth. But what they say amounts to the same thing. By making Mumbai a union territory, Nehru has beheaded Maharashtra. Now where is the head that we can keep cool although we are being constantly urged by Congressmen to do so. Today we find ourselves in a distressing situation. We do not have power. We do not have wealth. We do not have weapons. We do not have even newspapers. Last Sunday some eight lakh Marathi people had gathered in this park. But the *Times of India* did not as much as mention us. As against that, this shameless newspaper calls the gathering at Chowpatty of some ten or fifteen thousand people and as many policemen a meeting so gigantic the likes of which had never been witnessed before in the history of the city. [Cries of Shame Shame!] It is not enough to cry shame shame. The whole of Maharashtra should boycott this newspaper. [Loud applause] So that is how it is. Nobody is on our side, except justice and God. [Loud applause] That is why there should not be a vestige of doubt in our minds that we are going to win this battle. [Applause]

'Nehru sees everything we do as wrong. He calls our satyagraha a tamasha. "Anybody can get up, throw a few stones, go to jail and call himself a hero," he says. "That is what their satyagraha amounts to." This satyagraha which started in November last year with the Bhishmacharya of the Independence movement, Senapati Bapat, plunging into it, is this the satyagraha which he calls a tamasha? The satyagraha in which some two lakh of our people participated, including senior men of sixty and over and women from respectable homes, the satyagraha whose banners flew from Belgaum in the south to Delhi in the north, is this satyagraha a tamasha? [Applause]

'Please do not forget that Nehru's declaration regarding Mumbai has its source in Shankarrao Dev's head. [Much shaming of Shankarrao] Last November, did he not tell lakhs of people in this very place where I stand today that he would not continue to live even for a second longer if Mumbai was not given to us? In that case surely his avatar should have packed up and left this planet last Sunday. But no such luck. He is alive and kicking. [Prolonged laughter] Our Kakasaheb Gadgil is no different. What melodramatic slogans he raised. There will be another Indian war for a united Maharashtra, he said. Our weapons are ready on the shami tree he said. [Tremendous laughter] The fight for Bombay, he said in English, will be fought on the streets of Bombay. Who would have thought that an avatar of a Mahabharat warrior would one day take birth in a corner of Pune? [Laughter] And now, even when Nehru has declared unambiguously that Mumbai will be a union territory for the next five years, this "uncle" continues to say, "I can still see a ray of hope in Nehru's sense of justice." He sees a ray of hope in pitch darkness. If he goes to the crematorium—I mean on his own two feet—he might pick up a pinch of ash and say, "I still see signs of life here." [Two minutes of continuous laughter] Bhausaheb Hirey, Yashwantrao Chavan are all birds of the same feather. Their modus operandi is to make brave statements before us about revolting against the Congress and then tuck their tails in and prostrate themselves before its leaders.

'Some people say the Samyukta Maharashtra Movement cannot succeed because it lacks a leader. Do leaders fall from the sky? They are born out of agitations. The days for single leaders, a Tilak or a Gandhi, are past. They will never return. The time has now come for collective leadership. The Samiti which leads the united Maharashtra movement comprises five political parties—Communist, Praja Socialist, Socialist, Shetkari Kamgar and Hindutvavadi. This is a group of five Pandavas. These five Pandavas have the blessings of our deity, Chhatrapati Shivaji Maharaj. [Tremendous applause]'

It must be pointed out that while the five Pandavas stood together for the common cause, at least two went at each other hammer and tongs on the sidelines of the main battle, without letting their skirmish affect their commitment to it. These two leaders, both gifted with razor-sharp tongues and few inhibitions, were Keshav Sitaram Thackeray and P.K. Atre, residents of opposite sides of Shivaji Park. In a television interview, Bal Thackeray narrated the story of the skirmish which came to be known as the Thackeray–Atre Vaad (quarrel). Thackeray senior was founder-editor of *Prabodhan* (Enlightenment) a journal aimed at social reform. Atre was editor of the weekly *Navayug* and the daily *Maratha*, both published from his press in Worli. This prompted Thackeray to refer to him often as the Worli Pig. The skirmish began when some inconsequential third person happened to be visiting the older Thackeray with his godman guru, whoever he was. Atre happened to drop in and was introduced to the godman. Atre barely took notice of him. This incensed the devotee. He wrote an article in *Prabodhan* denouncing Atre. Atre thought Thackeray had written the article. He responded by describing Thackeray's style of journalism as Saraswati blowing a conch shell with one hand, and beating a drum with the other. Thackeray hit back, describing Atre's writing as the product of a pen dipped in a commode. More insults were traded, including Thackeray calling Atre 'a Communist with a dirty tongue'. With Thackeray's deep-seated animosity against Communists, this was the ultimate abuse in his bag of insults. From here on the quarrel spiralled till Atre decided to step back, announcing the end of hostilities from his side.

The fear in Nehru's cabinet that linguistic states would encourage linguistic chauvinism, soon proved to be justified in Maharashtra. Only a fine line divides proper pride from chauvinism. The Samyukta Maharashtra movement had created a constituency where linguistic identity and victimhood could be exploited for political power. Around the time that Maharashtra became a unilingual State with

Bombay as its capital, Bal Thackeray, still a resident of Shivaji Park, started a satirical magazine called *Marmik*. Translated for its sense, the name means bull's eye. In this case the bull's eye was the south Indian who had all the clerical jobs that the middle-class Maharashtrian aspired to. Thackeray gave the name 'Marathi manoos' to his constituency and 'Yandu gundus' to south Indians. Six years later on Dussehra day, 30 October 1966, Thackeray launched his party, the Shiv Sena, in Shivaji Park. On that day he also launched a campaign against south Indians with the slogan, 'Bajao pungi hatao lungi'. The enormous number of people who turned up at his first ever rally surprised Thackeray himself. After his incendiary speech, the expected happened. The incited mob dispersing from the rally attacked shops and restaurants owned by south Indians, looted them and set them on fire while the police stood by. The Shiv Sena thrived under the protection of Congress chief ministers and became all-powerful. Vijay Tendulkar saw this as a repeat of the Frankenstein story. He wrote his play *Ghashiram Kotwal* as a warning. But this Frankenstein won an important battle for his patrons. He ousted their prime enemy, the Communists, from their stronghold in the mill area of the city.

10. Heritage

A Sense of Place

'Creation of "a Sense of Place" is one of the most important attributes of a heritage precinct. This is created a) by a common built form and b) by a common history—cultural, political, economic. A built form is not just a cluster of buildings, but includes features like streets, foliage of trees, water bodies, open spaces or any special feature or icon of cultural significance. Even well-known personalities associated with the area contribute to the heritage significance. This array of tangible and intangible heritage attributes is evolved over a period of years by the collective energies of the local residents. "A Sense of Place" thus emerges out of a vibrant process. It then imparts a collective identity and a feeling of pride to the residents of the precinct.'

—*Final report,* Guidelines for the Conservation of Shivaji Park as a Heritage Precinct, *Adarkar Associates, consultants to The Mumbai Metropolitan Region–Heritage Conservation Society (MMR–HCS), April 2014.*

In the overlapping of turfs that forms an inescapable feature of how Indian states and cities are governed, the MMR–HCS is one of the players concerned with the conservation of Mumbai's heritage sites. The other player is the Brihanmumbai Municipal Corporation's Mumbai Heritage Conservation Committee (MHCC), which counts architects, historians, environmentalists and heritage activists among its members. This committee has been chaired in the past by eminent retired bureaucrats. The Adarkar Associates report cites the following definition of a heritage precinct from the MHCC—Revised Heritage Regulations [DCR 67] for Conservation of Heritage Sites for Greater Mumbai: 'A heritage precinct is an area of heritage value. It could consist of a number of buildings and spaces, such as streets, with cultural or heritage significance worth recognizing and conserving, or it could be an area where relationship between various elements create a special sense of place like mass, scale, building material, typology, roof profile and shapes or containing architectural style or elements. Precincts are of different importance and are made up of different type of elements such as houses, trees, commercial properties and public spaces combining to create a unique significance.'

MHCC's definition, besides being largely tautological, suffers from the kind of linguistic imprecision that can easily allow for semantic quibbling. Rules that are not precisely stated can be bent to mean other things. The Adarkar

Associates definition is clearly conceived and expressed. Its argument for making Shivaji Park a heritage precinct is convincing.

2014 was a critical year for Shivaji Park as a heritage precinct. There was much quibbling over nomenclature to allow the face-off between conservationists and the builders lobby to be resolved. In August–September 2012, news reports had announced that Shivaji Park had been listed as a heritage precinct. Precinct meant the park and the buildings facing it, variously numbered between 187 and 192. The reports explained that as residents, people would not only be responsible for maintaining the principal features of their homes such as façade and height, but would have to apply to the MHCC for permission even for minor repairs.

Instantly an enormous Maharashtra Navnirman Sena hoarding went up outside the eastern entrance to the park, demanding to know how the residents of Shivaji Park would feel if they were prohibited from hammering even a nail in their walls. The MNS chief, Raj Thackeray, is a real estate developer. A few days later his hoarding was replaced by a Shiv Sena hoarding also roaring its protest against the heritage tag for Shivaji Park buildings. The arguments that followed made it clear how little politicians knew or cared about heritage. 'With the exception of the Mayor's Bungalow,' they said, 'what is so architecturally great about the buildings around Shivaji Park that makes them worth preserving?' Prodded by politician-builders, residents too protested.

Taking cognisance of their protests, the BMC constituted a review committee under Dinesh Afzalpurkar, ex-chief secretary in the Shiv Sena–BJP government of 1995–99. The committee was tasked with visiting Shivaji Park to hear residents' objections and suggestions. It held two meetings with residents. On 14 September 2014, two reports regarding its recommendations appeared, one in *The Free Press Journal* and the other in *The Indian Express*. The headline of the first read 'Shivaji Park Still a Heritage Site'. But Shivaji Park's status had never been in question. 'In a relief to civic activists and environmentalists,' said the report, 'chairman of the Heritage Sites Review Committee Dinesh Afzalpurkar told *FPJ* on Saturday that Shivaji Park has not been struck out of the Heritage Sites list. Instead, it enjoys better protection under the newly created category of "heritage open space" as against its earlier status of "Grade I".' This report confused the issue unnecessarily. Believing these media reports, former municipal commissioners V. Ranganathan, D.M. Sukhtankar, Sharad Kale and Jamshed Kanga were reported to have 'registered their protest towards removing the heritage site status of the maidan'.

The Indian Express report clarified the issue. Far from being 'a relief to civic activists and environmentalists' as the *FPJ* report had claimed, Afzalpurkar's switching around of the definition of Shivaji Park had filled them with anxiety. The report quoted MHCC chairman V. Ranganathan as saying, 'Grade-I is the highest status that can be attributed to a heritage maidan like Shivaji Park. Lowering it from that status will only pave way for construction in that zone, which is one of the few surviving heritage spaces of the city. We have preserved Oval Maidan for so many years without allowing construction. Shivaji Park deserves the same status. Further, there is no such heritage category as "open space" and therefore no guidelines have been listed for it.'

Afzalpurkar admitted that his report had indeed recommended creating a new category of 'open space'; but he asserted that this nomenclature would be equivalent to the tag of Grade-I heritage status. He was quoted in *The Indian Express* report as stating, 'The new category of "open space" for Shivaji Park maidan will in no way permit any construction on it. We cannot continue to retain it in the Grade-I list because the category restricts development around 100m surrounding the area. It will hamper the re-development of the 187 buildings. For Grade-I heritage structures, as per section 67 of the Development Control Regulations, 1991, a buffer zone of 100 metres surrounding the structure is formed where the "view to" and the "view from" the said structure must be maintained.' So what he was saying in effect was that the park space had been redefined in order to allow buildings around it to be redeveloped. The builders' lobby had won.

Four years elapsed after the September 2014 reports before the heritage status of Shivaji Park reappeared in the news. A report in *The Indian Express* dated 9 October 2018 indicated that the Government had still not arrived at a decision regarding the heritage tag to be given to Shivaji Park. Was it to be 'open space' as recommended by the Afzalpurkar Committee or Grade-I Heritage as recommended by the V. Ranganathan-led Mumbai Heritage Conservation Committee? The Adarkar Associates' well-argued position for making the Shivaji Park precinct a heritage site because of its 'sense of place', seemed not to be under consideration at all. This was made amply clear in what a member of the Afzalpurkar committee told *The Indian Express*. 'We felt we cannot discriminate on the heritage grades for open spaces. Cooperage Maidan is as important as Shivaji Park Maidan or August Kranti Maidan. In these spaces, there is no clear distinction for being categorized as Grade-I or Grade-II, so instead it has been suggested that a new grade, "OS" be introduced for these. The new grade would mean only the open space has to be protected and preserved.' Had the Cooperage and the August Kranti Maidan precincts been planned as architecturally coherent neighbourhoods? Did these two 'open spaces' even match in the MHCC's own, albeit clunky, definition of a heritage precinct as incorporating 'different type of elements such as houses, trees, commercial properties and public spaces combining to create a unique significance'? If not, was their comparison with Shivaji Park valid?

In removing the precinct from the heritage tag, had the committee thought of a way in which its 'sense of place' could be preserved? The report answers this question with the information that the committee had recommended to the state government that it 'recognise the proposed precinct as an Area of Comprehensive Development under the Maharashtra Regional and Town Planning Act of 1996'. Presumably it is under this Act that the committee 'has proposed a height limit of 34–40 m for redevelopment projects in Shivaji Park. This is in line with final demands made by the group leaders of the BMC and the mayor at a meeting with Afzalpurkar in January. The new limit is opposed to the MHCC's guideline of a height limit of 24–30 m for redevelopment in heritage precincts.' The report goes on to say that builders will no longer be required 'to maintain balconies, a characteristic feature of the present precinct. The committee has suggested introducing Art Deco window grills instead of box grills. The broad recommendations do not provide any protection for specific structures in the precinct that are of markedly greater heritage value and design.'

We have come a long way from the simple definition of Shivaji Park inscribed in a commemorative pillar located on the kerb behind the Udyan Ganesh temple. The inscription reads: 'This public recreation ground which was opened for public use in 1925 has been called "Shivaji Park" in commemoration of the tercentenary of Shri Shivaji Maharaj by the order of the Municipal Corporation 1927'. The Marathi inscription that follows translates 'recreation ground' as 'kreedangan' that is playground. In defending its 'sanctity', activists have always used the description playground. Perhaps the phrase 'recreation ground' carries the danger of being defined as a ground for activities that need not be strictly sporting.

Saurab Rao

One of the many towers around Shivaji Park

Nomenclature is everything in the battle between development and conservation. In the case of Dadar Chowpatty we may say the battle is between development and preservation. Till August 2018, Dadar beach was called chowpatty like Girgaum chowpatty. The root of the word chowpatty is descriptive. It indicates a place where chow (four) pati (streams) come together. At some point of time the sea at Girgaum might have been the coming together of four creeks. One does not know when the streams or inlets or creeks merged to form a single expanse of sea. But the descriptive name stuck and became the accepted word for any sandy beachfront. Both Dadar and Juhu beaches are referred to as chowpattys. Had Dadar continued to be called chowpatty, suggesting an open sea, then it would have come under the Coastal Regulation Zone rules, preventing development of old buildings that fell within 500 metres of the High Tide Line (HTL). So the city fathers, ever willing to oblige developers, suddenly recalled that this beach was really part of Mahim Bay. Indeed it used to be called Mahim Bay in the old days. Once Dadar Chowpatty was renamed Mahim Bay, the rules around it changed. The cut-off line for redeveloping old buildings is now 100 metres instead of 500 from the HTL.

So that is where we stand. Well not quite. Because we still do not know whether our park is an open space or a Grade-I heritage site. The government is in no hurry to decide. Meanwhile, towers of varying height and design are sprouting up around the park, with builders taking full advantage of the 'open space' available between the review committee's recommendations and their ratification by the all-important Government Regulation (GR).

11. Morning Walk

18 February 2019

'Above all, do not lose your desire to walk: every day I walk myself into a state of well-being and walk away from every illness; I have walked myself into my best thoughts, and I know of no thought so burdensome that one cannot walk away from it.'

—Søren Kierkegaard in a letter to his niece, 1847

KIERKEGAARD SHOULD HAVE ADDED, 'MOST IMPORTANTLY, do not stop to talk while walking. Talking interferes with thinking. When you have done talking, your best thoughts have vanished.' That has been my experience. I have had many good thoughts during my regulation two rounds of Shivaji Park. I can vouch for the fact that creative juices flow like crazy when I am out there. Some of my columns and stories have taken shape as I have done the good old one-two one-two in the morning air. But Shivaji Park offers other pleasures too. One of them is trees, those that flank Keluskar Road and some that grow in the compounds of the homes that line it. Nobody seems to remember when the trees were planted. A group of students from the 2013–14 batch of Sophia Social Communications Media department have made a film on Shivaji Park in which an elderly resident recalls that sometime in the '70s, stumps appeared around the park overnight and grew into the trees we see today. This does not sound convincing. Moving hundred plus stumps from wherever they were to the park would have been a project of gigantic proportions involving careful digging out of the stumps with rootballs attached and replanting them in previously prepared holes; then tending to them till the roots took hold. No overnight work, this. It would have surely been easier to plant saplings. The BMC does that all the time when it replaces trees that have been uprooted by the monsoon wind and rain.

Whatever the origin of the kerbside trees, they now give us much visual pleasure all the year round as well as welcome shade in the summer months. We have peepals and rain trees, jambhul and gulmohars, copperpod and putranjeeva, banyans and Ashokas. Naturally, I have some favourites. The peltophorum behind the Shivaji statue stands so erect that a plumb line dropped from its proud head would fall exactly at its feet. Twice a year its delicate blossoms cover the pavement with a light lemon carpet. When it has no more flowers to shed, gleaming rusty-brown pods appear on its crown giving it its second name, copperpod. Behind Bengal Club is a copperpod that bends to cross the katta, merging with a desi badam that is growing outwards. There is such a confusion of trunks and leaves here that you wonder if desi almond leaves are growing out of a copperpod trunk until you give the combined canopy a good hard look. In the ever changing colour palette of the Shivaji Park periphery, the desi almond is a source of one of the most brilliant reds in nature. Today its leaves have turned into rubies hanging among emerald pendants, both washed over by the morning sun. Across the park a desi almond in a hurry is already a blaze of red.

There's another red that peeps out once in a while from a tall tree on the north side. This sterculia foetida, otherwise known as wild almond or java olive, is busy shedding leaves. Next month it will flower. One will then have to wait a full eleven months till next February for it to display its brilliant red fruit, hanging in clusters among its dense foliage. Soon the red will turn to black, split and scatter seeds on the pavement. It is a temperamental tree. There is a row of them in Bandra which are already bare of leaves with black fruit hanging like bats on their branches.

The magnificent old banyan beside the Scout Pavillion catches the morning sun amidships, so to say. Every last fibre of its trailing aerial roots is lit up today to a delicate russet while the trunk catches the cross light in each groove and ridge.

On the south side of the park, behind a handsome putranjeeva, hides a bakul tree. It announces its presence by the heavy scent of its tiny beige-brown flowers. You pick them up off the pavement, cup them in your palms and carry them home to scent your wardrobe. Further along in Raj Thackeray's Krishna Bhuvan compound stands a magnificent jackfruit tree. Last May, seven heavy fruit hung from its trunk, ready for the table. Currently, there is a media buzz around jackfruit in America. Foodies claim its flesh looks and tastes like pulled pork and is rich in calcium and potassium.

Saurab Rao

The katta welcomes dogs as much as human beings

The great rain trees are practically bare now, holding up their massive branches starkly to the sky. But by March they will put out tender green leaves and be crowned with delicate pink blossom.

The leaf-shedding season that we are in produces its own colours. The hues of the shed leaves go from lemon yellow to pale gold to bronze to copper and to a sienna so deep it verges on black. I've just picked up a champa leaf from the pavement and am marvelling at its fine, deeply etched veins, staggered along the central spine at so precise an angle, you wonder if there are protractors in nature. And the colour! How is one to describe it? Dark copper? On the surface it is that. But look deep and you see a vestigial green. Look deeper still and you catch a shade of old gold.

Walkers in the shade of an old banyan tree

An artist with all the pigments in the world at her disposal might still try in vain to recreate this amazing pentimento.

As varied as the trees are the people I pass. I know them all by face and by habit. Some people I understand. Others I do not. Here's the man who wears a baseball glove and cap as his walking dress. Here is another who trails a short stick along the railings enjoying the jaltarang-like music they produce. There is the advocate standing in his favourite spot near the Samarth Vyayam Mandir clapping vigorously. He once confided in me that he clapped to invite the crows. I have never seen a single crow accept his invitation. But he has not given up hope. The last two days he was done out of his pleasure. The Vyayam Mandir had erected a huge shamiana covering half the south side of the park for the first Mallakhamb World Championships held during the weekend of 16 and 17 February. Fifteen nations from Asia and Europe are reported to have participated. This is a huge feather in Uday Deshpande, our Mallakhamb ambassador's, cap.

And here is the man who once carried his possessions in a huge bag on his back when he came for a walk. He wanted me to write about his plight. His landlord was trying to evict him in order to redevelop the property. He has not been carrying his bag lately. Perhaps he has moved to another place. I cannot believe that any poor tenant in Shivaji Park can win against a landlord bent on redeveloping his property.

As I pass by the ajoba-ajji udyan on the east side, I hear a commotion. I notice my stalker at its centre. Yes of course, I have a stalker, I at eighty and he two years older. We were once colleagues in a south Bombay college. Keen to build on that acquaintance, he stops his Wagon R and honks when he sees me walking to the park. He wants to give me a lift. I ignore his honking. I have noticed that he has grown his hair and tosses it in sprightly fashion. He reminds me of the Surekha Punekar lavni: 'The leaf is ready to fall but the stalk is still green.'

Round the corner from the pest, there is compensation. Pt Shankar Abhyankar sits on the north katta with his music-loving friends. A few months ago he gave me a lift home to play me a bandish in Raga Deskar which he had composed and sung for a few select rasikas at Kumar Gandharva's request. It was a pleasure to begin the morning with his alaap and quicksilver taans regaling the ear.

There are other pleasures for the ear in Shivaji Park—the sound of many tongues. I count them today. I hear Marathi, Gujarati, Kutcchi, Sindhi, Kannada, Konkani and Bambaiyya Hindi. Not so pleasant is Minglish. Today's line was 'Mi recently aikla, to continuous bolat hota.' (I heard him recently. He was talking continuously.)

Shivaji Park still exudes 'a sense of place'. But the lovely, white-painted, single-storey Makhanwala House, once Shivaji Park's showpiece, is now rubble with an indifferent earth-mover standing on top of the heap. And as I turn the corner to return home, I wince to see the expanse of an impossible blue that swathes the lower floors of the tower across the road. The two-storeyed Prabhat with its graceful galleries stood here once. Now the parking floors of this tower throw their turquoise offence in our eyes.

Shivaji Park was once a commons where villagers met. It became a modern precinct where a unique culture grew. You looked across Shivaji Park then and saw trees. Now you see towers dwarfing the trees. 'One life was ending and another pulsating into being,' said S.N. Pendse about the Dadar of the early 1930s. One might use the same line to describe what is happening to Shivaji Park today. But for all you know, history will describe this as progress. Which, if I can repress my nostalgia and preoccupation with heritage, I should admit it is.

Bibliography

Devidayal, Namita. *The Music Room*. Penguin Random House India, 2008.

Dhuru, Vasumati. *Kashinath Devji Dhuru ani Suryavanshi Kshatriya Dnyati Samaj*. Granthali, 2014.

Dwivedi, Sharada and Mehrotra, Rahul. *Bombay: The Cities Within*. India Book House Pvt. Ltd, 1995.

Guidelines for Shivaji Park Heritage Precinct for MMR–Heritage Conservation Society, Final Report, April 2014.

Iyer, Kamu. *Bo(o)mbay: From Precincts to Sprawl*. Popular Prakashan Pvt. Ltd, 2014.

Jog, Leela N. *Women Pioneers of Catering Education and Consumer Movement*. Bharatiya Vidya Bhavan, 1994.

Kamat, Prakash with Raut, Sandeep and Patil, Vikas (Eds). *Bahurangi Bahudhangi Dadar*. Datta Dinanath Kamthe for Dadar Sarvajanik Vachanalaya, 2007.

Keshavacharya and Others, V.K. Rajwade (Ed.). *Mahikavatichi urf Mahimchi Bakhar*. Chitrashala Press, Shaka 1846 (1924 CE).

Kulkarni, Jayant Vitthal. *Shivaji Parkchya Kattyavarun*. Self-published on the net.

Patel, Sujata and Thorner, Alice (Eds). *Bombay: Metaphor for Modern India* and *Bombay: Mosaic of Modern Culture*. Oxford University Press, 1995.

Pendse, Shri Na. *Kalandar*. Majestic Publishing House, 1959.

Rajadhyaksha, Mangesh Vitthal. *Nivadlele Kharde*. Mouj Prakashan Gruha, 2013.

Rao, Nikhil. *House But No Garden: Apartment Living in Bombay's Suburbs, 1898-1964*. University of Minnesota Press, 2013.

Ratna, Kalpish. *Room 000—Narratives of the Bombay Plague*. Pan Macmillan India, 2015.

Sanzgiri, Dwarkanath. *Dadar Ek Pinakolada*. Majestic Publishing House, 2014.

Sardar, G.B. with Karve, C.G., Shikhare, D.N. and Panse, M.G. (Eds). *Maharashtra-Jeevan: Parampara, Pragati ani Samasya, Vols 1 and 2*. Messrs Joshi ani Lokhande Prakashan, 1960.

Shah, Amrita. *Ahmedabad: A City in the World*. Bloomsbury, 2015.

The Great Son of Vaitarna. Modak Smarak Samiti, 2013.

Tindall, Gillian. *City of Gold: Biography of Bombay*. Penguin Books, 1992.

ALSO IN SPEAKING TIGER

Chandni Chowk

The Mughal City of Old Delhi

Swapna Liddle

'A wonderful and much-needed introduction to the history of the Old City of Delhi and a welcome addition to the literature on Shahjahanabad.'—William Dalrymple

What we know today as Chandni Chowk was once a part of one of the greatest cities of the world—the imperial city established by the Mughal emperor Shahjahan in the seventeenth century, and named after him—Shahjahanabad. This is the story of how the city came to be established, its grandeur as the capital of an empire at its peak, and its important role in shaping the language and culture of North India. It is also the story of the many tribulations the city has seen—the invasion of Nadir Shah, the Revolt of 1857, Partition.

Today, Shahjahanabad has been subsumed under the gigantic sprawl of metropolitan Delhi. Yet it has an identity that is distinct. Popularly known as Chandni Chowk, its name conjures up romantic narrow streets, a variety of street food and exotic markets. For Shahjahanabad is still very much a living city, though the lives of the people inhabiting it have changed over the centuries. Dariba Kalan still has rows of flourishing jewellers' shops; Begum Samru's haveli is now Bhagirath Palace, a sprawling electronics market, and no visit to Chandni Chowk is complete without a meal at Karim's, whose chefs use recipes handed down to them through the ages for their mouth-watering biriyani and kebabs.

Swapna Liddle draws upon a wide variety of sources, such as the accounts of Mughal court chroniclers, travellers' memoirs, poetry, newspapers and government documents, to paint a vivid and dynamic panorama of the city from its inception to recent times.

Page Extent: 196 pp | Price: ₹499

ALSO IN SPEAKING TIGER

Connaught Place

and the Making of New Delhi

Swapna Liddle

'The value of this book is that it interweaves the familiar story of how New Delhi was built, with social history and reflections on the future of the capital city. An excellent introduction for both inhabitants and visitors.'—Narayani Gupta, Historian

The origin of New Delhi can be traced to the Coronation Durbar in December 1911, where Emperor George V announced the transfer of the capital of the British Empire in India from Calcutta to Delhi.

Swapna Liddle traces in fascinating detail the events that led up to that historic day: the deliberations over the choice of location; the roles played by the Viceroy, Lord Hardinge, and the two principal architects, Edwin Lutyens and Herbert Baker; and, finally, the naming of the capital as 'New Delhi'—to distinguish it from the old city of Shahjahanabad.

Even as the new capital took shape, it was Connaught Place that gave life to the city. Designed as a shopping and commercial centre for the elite—both British and Indian—it boasted of the most exclusive shops, cinemas and restaurants.

While many of the old familiar haunts like Gaylord, Volga and Regal Cinema have shut their doors, Connaught Place continues to reinvent itself with shiny new multiplexes, branded stores and restaurants taking their place. A guidebook of the early 1940s described Connaught Place as 'indeed the most fashionable shopping centre…and, undoubtedly the most progressive part of the most progressive town in the country.' The crowds that continue to throng its corridors, both young and old, visitors to the city and residents alike, bear testimony to the statement.

Page Extent: 196 pp | Price: ₹499

ALSO IN SPEAKING TIGER

Thamel

Dark Star of Kathmandu

Rabi Thapa

'A moody, elegant portrait of an emblematic neighbourhood as it has changed through time... This is a richly storied book, and one that captures the energy and verve of contemporary Kathmandu.'—Manjushree Thapa

For long a sleepy rural enclave, Thamel is today the beating commercial and cultural heart of Kathmandu—a dizzying square kilometre of hotels, bars, cafés, bookshops and temples to which visitors and residents gravitate, drawn by its dazzle and its possibilities.

In this unusual biography of the place, Rabi Thapa revisits the haunts of his youth. Tramping around its temples and monasteries, he unravels its layered history as well as the tales of the kings, monks and travelling merchants who laid its foundations. From residents—both Nepali and those who visited and never left—he pieces together the story of Kathmandu of the 'flower-power' sixties, the legendary Freak Street, and the rise of modern Thamel. On its streets he encounters glue-sniffing children, local toughs battling for turf, transvestite prostitutes turning tricks, and entrepreneurs looking to make it big. What emerges is a finely detailed portrait of a place that is not only a vibrant, ever-evolving reflection of the social mores of Kathmandu, but also an enduring staging post for Western fantasies of the East.

Written in the best traditions of flânerie, *Thamel* combines history, memoir and sharp reportage to tell the electric story of a place forever in flux, forever reinventing itself to suit the appetites and desires of those who seek it out.

Page Extent: 184 pp | Price: ₹399